Ghostly Embers:
Visions of Toledo

Copyright © 2005 Larry Rochelle
All rights reserved.
ISBN: 1-4196-0455-4

To order additional copies, please contact us.
BookSurge, LLC
www.booksurge.com
1-866-308-6235
orders@booksurge.com

Ghostly Embers:
Visions of Toledo

Poems

Larry Rochelle

2005

Ghostly Embers: Visions of Toledo

CONTENTS

Blue Night Madness	1
Part 1 Blue Streak Edition	3
West Toledo Newsboy	4
Triage on the High-Level Bridge	5
Monroe Street Twisted Mister	7
Payment Due on Madison Avenue	8
Point Place Ice Storm	9
Ghostly Embers	10
Cops and Robbers	11
Imbroglio on Upton	12
Plaskon Nightmare	13
Winter on Freeman Street	15
Dad's Willys	16
Plastic Bubbles	17
Annie Eye Over	18
Cordon at Calvary	19
Late Night: Walden Pond	20
Sentry on Kenwood	21
Purple Gang Shoot-Out	23
TU Tower	24
Sit on the Table, Pops ...	25
Near Ottawa Park, 1953	26
Duck and Cover	27
Walter Winchell Fear	28
Psychic Terror	29
White Hut Pulse	30
Black Sweat	31
Peephole near Kresge's	32
Glass Bowl Rumble	33

Holy Toledo   35
West End Grid   36
Gutter Tag   37
Polio Fog: 1950   38
Blue Streaks at Dawn   39
Part 2 The Peach Page   45
Haunted Leaves on Torrey Hill   46
A&P Surrealism   47
Christmas Eve: 1954   48
Christmas Morning: 1951   49
Sirens Rise   50
Two-Car Garage   51
Sonic Booms   52
Ottawa Tavern Aftermath   53
Along the Tracks   54
Barbershop Jig   55
Little Red Wagon   56
Bank Nite at the Colony   57
The Cat That Cried Dead Kittens   58
Artie Shaw Summer   59
Lunch at Plaskon: 1947   60
The Back Room   61
Pond-Crack at Walden   62
Oak Openings Hummingbirds   63
Black Clouds at Reno Beach   64
Centennial Jazz   65
Mood Indigo   66
Bargain City Grand Opening   67
Fairmont Pharmacy Fire   68
Brush-Off at the Art Museum   69
Dad's Pall Malls   70
Thimbles at the Gallery   71

Plastic Desperation   72
At the Peristyle   73
War and Peace   74
Libbey Court Ghost   75
Ottawa River Romance   76
Blizzard near St. Anthony's   77
Reverie   78
The Porch on Freeman   79
Parade down Madison   80
Downtown Pub Crawl   81
She Spoke Soup   82
Before Tiedke's Burned   83
Colony Matinee: 1953   84
A Free Man   85
Caboose Yellow at the Lion's Store   86
Cherry Street Love   87
Auction on Junction   88
To Waterville   89
After Reading the Peach Page   91
Angels at Toledo Hospital   92
Club Cherry   93
Lipstick Smear Gallery   94
The Personals   95
Pulse   96
Thoughts during Lent   97
Mistletoe at Ma's   98
Gesu Midnight Mass   99
Gesu Recess   100
Purple Gang Visitation   101
Woodlawn Cemetery   103
Tree Lot on Alexis   105
Perrysburg I-Hop Crush   106

Smooth Jazz—ooks! 107
Rocky's on Telegraph 108
East Harbor Cellulite 109
Ten Mile Creek 110
Cold Fingers 111
The Silk Robe 112
Ducks at Crane Creek 113
Going to War 114
Jerry Springer Visits the Mall 115
Red Wells Opus No. 35 117
Cocoons in Side-Cut Park 118
Ottawa Park Amphitheater 119
Locust Song at the Zoo 121
Sculpture at the Glass Pavilion 122
Night Antics 123
Bins of Beauty at Boogie 124
Snap 125
"B" Movie Review 126
Part 3 Opinion Page 131
Cold Times 133
Security Moms 138
Say Your Prayers 139
Toledo Grid 140
Welfare Department 141
Right-Wing Education 142
Scapegoats for Right-Wing Wrath 143
Horror 144
Disdain for Hollywood 145
Why Peter Slept 146
A Jack Dempsey Moment 147
Blind and Narrow 148
Neocons 149

After the Election   151
Impeach Him   152
City Council   153
Oil   154
No Birth Control Today   156
Presidential Pardon   158
Mart-Mart   160
Iraq Flashback   161
Iraqi Kids   163
Nuclear Clock   165
Thirsting for Oil   166
Oh, Holy Night   167
Part 4 Sports Page   173
Darts at Ottawa Park   174
Visit 175
We Meet Sports Guy   176
Eight Ball   177
Homeruns at The Dump   178
Fort Meigs Sport   180
Mud Hen Baseball   181
Morning Jog at Wildwood   182
Ottawa Hills Tennis   183
Aurora at Fremont Speedway   184
Battle at the Paintball Coliseum   185
Fast-Pitch Softball   186
CYO Football   187
The Cave on North Cove   188
Old-Timer at Jermain   189
Nocturnal Sport   190
Ace, The Friendly Dog   191
Yearbook Mob   192
Hunter's Perch   193

Ottawa Park Sledding   194
Jermain Park Industrial League   195
Getting to Westminster   196
POETRY: 207

To the good sisters of Gesu School, the Oblates at St. Francis, the University of Toledo, Johnson County Community College, the circulation department of THE TOLEDO BLADE, and the magnificent caretakers of Ottawa Park and Jermain Park.

Blue Night Madness

not for others
do poets write,
their minds churning
for pithy words
so exact that mind-
meld streaks with
bright sun's delight.

no, poets search internal
engines for truth-
telling on their own
watch,
keeping themselves,
honest,
telling themselves,
to be exact.
assuring their own psyche
quietude,
so blue night madness does not
steal their souls.

***

Part 1 Blue Streak Edition

I grew up on the west side of Toledo, near Upton and Bancroft.
At that time we had Fairmont Pharmacy, a barber shop,
a meat market/grocery, a bakery, Ottawa Tavern,
a shoe store and a sundry store on that corner,
along with Stutz's gas station. My friends and I worked
on that corner, picking up our bundles of Toledo Blades
outside Fairmont Pharmacy and delivering them
to the neighborhoods to the north of that corner.
I had the four p.m. "Home Edition."
The "Blue Streak" edition came at about five-fifteen,
right at sunset in the winter.

***

West Toledo Newsboy

not too surprising, but
many young boys
rely on newspaper delivery jobs
for cash, tossing paper missiles
on porches in small town
America where moms still bake
cod for supper,
waiting till later to read
headlines about Borneo, wondering
with whimsy, if neutered cows still lactate,
hoping that mad cow milk still
promises hope for calcium starved
lads who come home to
dads waiting and hoping
for beef, chicken
and pig to regulate
their hearts and get
them all to heaven.

Triage on the High-Level Bridge

not one of us was hurt,
the car's bent frame
leaning heavily over the edge,
its exhaust still sputtering
a putt-putt tune,
windshield wipers furiously
beating a window
completely cracked, gone,
yet
wipers flailed at invisible
water droplets,
and ambulances arrived
on the bridge, bright red lights,
seen for miles,
reflected off dark waters
down the river toward
the smell of fish, but we leaned on
pillows of light cast
against the police
car, a dark shroud of hope,
our quest for life saved
to breathe through
oxygen masks,
not so much for life,
not so much for fear,
but mostly for our
conception, and we
thanked out mothers
for giving birth,

thanked our fathers for that
life spurt that might have
but didn't crack this tumbling
night, our own car
flipped over
in murky water.

Monroe Street Twisted Mister

locked out again,
our neighbor prowled
the cold night,
ready for a light.
his smoke curled past
the porch, his uplifted
cigarette complained
against the full moon,
while his wife
peered
out,
her mini-blinds revealing
bright eyes
and a smirk.
he commenced to pounding
some secretive marital code,
a deadly beat against the door
so primitive it brought
the forest wolf, his sharp teeth
bared, his howl
loud, and Joyce our
neighborhood watcher
shimmied up
the light pole,
calling
the police swat team,
bright moon casting
their dark shadows
across our patio.

Payment Due on Madison Avenue

the temperature of blood's dynamics
pulsates inside, the morning light
somewhere over the Atlantic.
and one appointment early
the next day seems condensed
in sleepless futures,
always being a contraption
for pain.
touch it with your tongue,
it bursts. swallow the fever
of worry, focus on smiles,
but giddy laughter releases
the horror.
the clock ticks,
toilet water drips,
the agony of one more hour
sucked out of tomorrow
and when will you pay it back?

Point Place Ice Storm

hangers they're called
by some, those leftovers
after winds and ice molest the
plains, the flotsam
of storms too big
for video capture.

these hangers linger, hiding
at forty feet, swaying
with each new moon,
hanging and swinging
above.

few watch, few wait
for limb to fall; humans
mow their lawns, plant roses
sensing sun's heat.

when they fall, hangers
glide like geese
waiting for splash time,
a swish, a feeling of doom;
no one tells the child
to move,
no one sees limbs fall,
but thumps bring
parents to windows
and children have no time
to look.

Ghostly Embers

turning, gyrating,
bright burning bits ignite flares,
destructive, deadly.

Cops and Robbers

Near the corner of Upton and Milburn was an old garage.
Each time I went past there, I got a shiver.
According to my dad's recollection, there had been
a big shoot-out there between the cops and
an organized crime gang. A few were killed,
and in my imagination I could see them
crouching beside that garage, firing their pistols.

Imbroglio on Upton

gunfire in the night,
a passing car speeds,
its occupants
laughing, taking
video images.

nocturnal vandals
on the march,
storm troopers
for retaliation.

bullets whistle
through windows,
striking flesh,
babies cry.

doctors suture
wounds gaping,
souls shiver,
waiting for death.

Plaskon Nightmare

it could be something small,
a window crashing too loudly,
a piece of fish lodged
against the back
of the ice chest; these moments
clasp muscles tight,
make bedsprings hard,
the sound of mother's feet
cuddling the rug,
as if they'd strangle bedclothes
from the crib.

the bars seem wider than
remembered,
each wooden slat piercing
concrete then arcing
to ceilings,
our fingers pushing
through openings, grasping for air,
     but the breezes fail us,
lifting dust bunnies
and tiger lily petals
from the floor and
tossing them lightly on footstools.

after, no one talks;
how could they?
these hints of hopelessness
are rated adult; only those

older might see these shadows;
only our father
might lift us up,
over the slats and into
his strong, factory arms,
more used to gears,
pulleys and grease,
than baby's bottoms
swathed in Vaseline.

Winter on Freeman Street

toes knew when to visit,
not long after the storm but
before the hot coffee
could be poured, the nightly
paper stashed inside
by the couch
after its
thump would hit the porch door,
hard,
then, then, the toes
would linger on the vent,
absorbing
warm coal-heat,
forced up from below,
its coal-smell fitting
nicely with the mint of cocoa
for the kids, mom's coffee
still bubbling in its
canister on the gas stove,
and father slamming the door
to the Willys just
before stomping into
the entryway, taking
off his gloves
touched by frost,
throwing them
down upon the carpet,
flinging frost
across the tiles.

Dad's Willys

Ottawa Park was less than a block away from
1924 Freeman where I lived on the lower
duplex with my parents, my brother, Bob
and my sister, Barb. Dad had an old gray Willys
with the driver's side window out. He
covered it with part of a rug. It drove
nice. It was about a
1939 model. We'd go for rides in the
evening out west to the railroad tracks,
sit on the hood of the Willys until a
train came by. It was our biggest thrill at that time.

Plastic Bubbles

monsters quiet for once,
the tuning forks ringing alarms,
but most noticed little,
their intake of air
still viable,
their shouts subdued;
and for the others,
no breathing problems,
but, locally, air intake
seemed below par,
each one rising,
enclosed in plastic
for flight;
nearby, other workers
toyed with frigid
granules,
food stored ingeniously
beneath cockpits,
ready in an instant
to be dissolved;
but spaceflight remains
mysterious,
expensive, each bubble
of air priceless,
each numbing space-drug
pulsating through veins
for years, and explosive
forces speeding across
the vacuum that is.

Annie Eye Over

odd, something inside
speeding like a ghost
sent from relatives long dead;
something ticking there,
a message sent from dad,
something not right,
a weakness and the stairs
seem deeper, steeper,
like a slow-motion fall
to oblivion.

Cordon at Calvary

those at the bottom
wondered,
death or life?
each quizzical notion
caused pain,
a willingness to fly
if necessary,
anything to lift
heavy wings toward
light.
but body weight lures
senses to dust,
each step
repelled instantly,
no one moving,
just the weight
of death
spiraling down.

Late Night: Walden Pond

keeping track of dizziness,
we embrace the cosmos,
vast and sage,
looming lovingly like white
orchids on a pond,
spinning in black liquid,
clear and lucid
to the eyes,
its formless searching
locks the skies
and eyeballs us
besides.

Sentry on Kenwood

I watched for prowlers
in the night.
Underneath the second floor balcony,
they came, littering
our flower beds
with ink-stained underpants,
flattened cans of Pepsi dotting
the barren sandy soil.

You watched me too,
looking down the eaves,
seeing my cold breath
against the moon,
the ocean groaning
its background tune.

Should I invite them up?
I asked. But your puzzled
frown, a faked innocence,
stopped me.

I knew your friends were bold,
but your own promises
hurt. So what
if they clambered down
the steps when I approached?
I could see things.
I felt things.

Did you think their bronzed
muscles turned invisible,
as their loins glistened
with more than dew?
Could I not see your fingerprints,
glowing on their inner thighs?

Purple Gang Shoot-Out

Union Station jammed with black marias ,
something about those 35 mm
cameras, snapping at midnight,
each shot revealing intruders, criminals,
those who break & enter our homes,
our suburban oases.
each citizen angry now, slamming car doors,
hurrying past the litter
of Kodak boxes piled along
sidewalks, each citizen holding
a camera, wanting instant film documentation of evil.
but overworked camera experts
steal time for sales, pushing new cameras,
new options, instead of dealing
with photos so gruesome, so revealing,
that camera sales have multiplied
like baby spiders in gray birthing sacs.

TU Tower

such is the human mind that,
when the elevator lurched,
the thirteen bodies tilted musically,
stereo cell phones ricocheted,
each clicked on, playing…
playing strange mood pieces from Iran,
songs of praise that at times seemed
more… more like a plea
for boysenberry marmalade, a purple
instinct, a rush, and folks grabbed garments
tighter, seeing for an instant
a funeral, a fun-fest
of collapsed tables at some
renegade celebration,
placing game show hosts in embarrassing
locations for days,
asking them to leap from observatories when stars
crushed solar systems,
and roentgens flashed through skin,
leaving survivors weeping for rain.

Sit on the Table, Pops ...

then inch closer to the edge,
placing your head just so, the floppy
stale towel gingerly linked to neck muscles,
and lean your throat back,
exposing its lines to the machine.

try not to flinch as electricity speeds
molecules deep inside, your
thyroid exposed as a gambler
with little need for dice.

you play this game poorly,
and your impenetrable force,
so scared inside,
will reek from cancer fear
and no one will hold your hand
even when the switch clicks off.

Near Ottawa Park, 1953

fearful separation
between earth and sky,
some gigantic swooping
of molecules,
warm and moist,
a seizure,
a sneeze,
a feeling of awe,
something not quite right,
a sampling, a gyration
both in universe
and satellite
and people feel
different
their hands enlarging,
their systems
decaying,
gaining a deeper knowledge
of death.

Duck and Cover

I participated in the "duck and cover" drills
during the 1950s at Gesu School.
Atomic warfare was in the news every day,
and my imagination was horrified by the huge
mushroom cloud I had watched on TV.
The cold war was very real. Each night I looked
up at the sky to the west, and if dark clouds rose up,
I feared the atomic bomb was on its way.
I had persistent nightmares of destruction,
often measuring the miles to Detroit, to Cleveland,
to Chicago, wondering if Toledo would be hit
by bombs in those cities. Radiation was also
a constant fear. Little did I realize that our
own atomic tests on the Yucca Flats might
be depositing Strontium 90 on Toledo. Friendly fire

Walter Winchell Fear

if there be pride
in holding our senses
lightly,
our own abilities
swaying within tight circles,
might we not portray meanings
off-kilter at best?
might we not shout
those phrases to the sky
and bring down tumults
both of brain
and body?
yet we sit,
instead, our microphones
clicked off,
our sizeable banks
of knowledge,
our arithmetic connections
simmering, settling
for so much less
than hoped.

Psychic Terror

enhanced we are at times,
the split inside
rendered moot,
so we become integrated,
each psychic split molded
once again,
no cleavage,
our movements smooth,
those thoughts caught
on table tops
or slipping off cold, white plates
now hanging together,
as if God wanted
one not two,
unity not male,
not female,
the universe one big shout
telling the answer
we long for each morning
as we wake.

White Hut Pulse

vacuum noise at first covers
the sounds of car exhausts, the suction
coming from an open window,
where non-native speakers say hello
into boxed voice machines, creating a buzz
of syllables unintelligible
and our order gets lost
in translation, the hamburger arriving
in a muffin, our cherry coke mushed
together with a malt,
each package leaking, dripping sugary
droplets on leather seats,
each micro-dotted chicken nugget
splashed with mustard, while the vacuum
pulsates and sucks our arms, our legs,
through the car window,
splattering us against the money counter
where our ears and noses fill up
with catsup from ruptured plastic bags
the size of sappy meals.

Black Sweat

When I was about ten, I got my first bike,
red naturally, from Western Auto on
Sylvania Avenue. Dad couldn't get it
inside the trunk, so I rode it home.
It seemed a very long ride. My hands
turned black from the nervous sweat
wearing away the rubber handles.
Later, after it had been in the weather
many years, I painted it yellow using
house paint. It was a mean machine,
leaning against the house near the side door.

Peephole near Kresge's

night's oceans underneath,
the men came to see,
loving ersatz lingo
so all could peer,
though no one knew
when the rift would open;
all were numbed
with intelligence,
eager to look
and they saw new worlds;
each day the lorries would pull,
latches would open and
cement would pour,
old buildings quaking with the heft,
oozing with new liquid,
and the men, older now and wearing hats,
would bend, their backs struggling
to hold steady,
their eyes pinched
and cracked to see,
the ladders long and wooden,
seeming to be miles below,
and each workman wore
his red bandanna across
one eye, their strong
arms lifting wheelbarrows,
dumping liquid granules
into the pit.

Glass Bowl Rumble

battering on windows,
eerie scrapings on siding,
the thump of laughter
when lights shine.

it's another night
in the new neighborhood,
teens dancing like ghouls
in streetlights,
obscenities soap-scrawled
on car windows.

school again with strangers,
moving in tough.
no summer chance to brawl,
maybe set things right.

territorial imperative,
they were here first.
friendly banter, nonsense,
evil at the core.

who sets these rules?
no one.
who moderates hatred?
some primitive pulse.

midnight's restless,
looking for a fight,

but cowards strike
at innocence
and brooding revenge
no help into the night.

Holy Toledo

pose the question:
when?
if those severe
headaches come,
blazing hot funk
spreading though eyeballs,
and the reaching out
ignored
by long-time friends,
their own
inhibitions stopping
responses,
while messy situations
cancel the years,
when faithful
and loyal
were more than
platitudes
but meant
friendship
not support groups,
and issues
were problems to be
solved.

West End Grid

if we looked at lives
from skies so blue,
if we fled to clouds
to watch our ghosts
walk by,
we'd see some patterned filigree,
a trace of human flame,
its cutting sharp
in neighborhoods,
but captured by intent.
we'd plot this course
like scientists,
observing strange life forms
and conquer hurtful memories
questing fulsome noise.
tiny human beings,
so vastly proud and poised,
remain just filaments
of movement
when traced from heights
so blue.

Gutter Tag

My street, Freeman Street, was not very wide,
but wide enough for the game of gutter tag.
On one side of the street would be the others.
I would be 'it.' Seven against one.
Until I tagged someone, it would be chaos.
They would all be trying to outrun me, or
whoever was it. Eventually it was seven
against one again. Then the game was over when
the last guy was tagged. Game over, another
one would begin with the first one caught being 'it.'

Polio Fog: 1950

summer and heat
sticky enough to doom
cicadas, their warbling
hisses rising steady
as the day meets the impossible.

killer bugs, smaller
than fingernails, land
delicately on knees,
on elbows, anywhere
a swat can be dodged.

so the trucks move out,
old pick-ups equipped with
hissing white fog,
and warning lights to
scare children back inside
homes tightly packed,
so poison kills
the flying buzzes,
their wicked needle noses
poised to strike skin,
but DDT flops them
dead.

***

Blue Streaks at Dawn

The morning of the fire I had been rearranging my work room. Most of the old Blue Streak newspapers I had saved from the War were yellowing, and pieces from the edges were falling on the floor near the heating grate between the book shelf and the window overlooking the street.

Rearranging really meant cleaning to my wife who was busy downstairs running the vacuum, even though it was just five a.m. and the only sound I heard, anyway, was the sound of sirens coming down Monroe Street toward the park. I never understood why they had to use sirens at five a.m. since most everyone was sleeping, especially on Saturday, so what was the point?

My wife. Yes. She got on these binges sometimes, like the time she woke me up at three a.m. one early morning after I had been stressed out at work all week and was too tired to even change my clothes before I went to bed.

She woke me at three a.m. telling me that "we have to talk."

She goes on these cleaning binges too, like today. I smelled the coffee on at about four a.m., so I had to pee anyway, and I got up and looked downstairs and she looks up at the same time and our eyes meet and she says, "We've got to clean."

So I pee and I go down to the kitchen, grab a cup of coffee, with cream and two spoons of sugar, and I say to my wife, "Okay, let's clean after I drink my coffee."

Before I get done she starts moving furniture,

getting the vacuum out of the closet and turning it on. There's dust everywhere, at least I think there is, so I move myself up to my room where I can think and wake up out of the dusty air.

She yells up, "You can start on your room if you wanna."

I shout down, "Fine with me."

But then I just sat there a while wondering why I have to start all this cleaning so early on my day off?

Then I noticed all the god-damn newspapers and special editions about the end of the War which I've been saving for the kids to peruse once we have any, and when they're old enough to read or be interested in the god-damn War, which I doubt there ever will be, either born or interested in the War. But the newspapers are getting old now since they've been sitting right above the heater and all and coal fires do burn hot, so I guess the fire hazard of it all got me thinking that maybe that's the place to start cleaning today.

And the sirens on Monroe Street zoomed down onto Auburn Avenue and they seemed to be heading right for our house, but I know we don't have no fire here so it must be someplace else, like maybe the stores on the corner of Upton and Bancroft? Maybe that's where they're goin?

So I tried to see out my window to the east; I thought maybe I could see a fire engine or something 'cause, geez they seemed so close.

And now Jill, that's my wife's first name, she starts hollering up the steps, "Jesus, Frank, those fire engines are right down the street."

I thought to myself why the fire engines have to be

on my street 'cause now I'm interested in where the god-damn fire is, so I look for my shoes and slip them on and fumble with the laces and finally shout down to Jill that I'm goin out to see where that

fire is at.

I clambered down the stairs, putting on my thick flannel shirt with the extra lining, because I noticed all the windows have frost on them so it must be really, really cold out and I had the sudden thought that this is a bad time for a fire for anyone, since Christmas is just three days away on next Tuesday.

And when I opened the front door, god almighty, the smell of smoke was so strong I thought my neighbor Phil's house was on fire. But no, it was up the street about two blocks away where I could hear the sirens whirring down to a stop, leaving only the blink-blink, blink-blink of their flashing lights to pulse out into the smoky dark morning.

Shit, I thought to myself. *Phil's already up at the corner watching the fire* and I also saw old Mr. Biner, the guy at the corner who always gets in trouble with the neighborhood kids when he keeps all the baseballs and softballs and tennis balls that land in his backyard. That old geezer is so stubborn he doesn't care what they do to him or his yard; he still keeps them damn balls even after the kids stomped on all his rose bushes last summer and ate all of his raspberries. Me and Jill just shake our heads and have to admit that old Mr. Biner has a lot of balls, if you get my meaning.

So I finally pull up to Phil who's entranced by the flames poppin' out of the drugstore roof. He's so tranced up he doesn't see me; he doesn't hear me for a minute or two. I'm yelling over the noise of wind and fire and sirens, "Hey, Phil, you ' fool. How'd this fire get started?"

Finally, Phil turns to me, his eyes reflecting the red-orange fire, and he says, "I don't know. I just got here."

So we watch and watch and the firemen are attacking the damn fire from every angle imaginable. Some are on the bakery roof, some are on ladders, some stand toward the front, shooting huge streams into the drug store, past the broken windows, train sets, perfume bottles, cologne bottles, after shave, and knocking the huge display of Lucky Strikes to smithereens.

And we have to step back a little as two more fire engines pull up and start to roll hose out over the street. The firemen have to run about two blocks down Upton Avenue to hook up with another hydrant and Phil and I watch as they make their mad scramble down the street, getting there out of breath, yet connecting the hose and cranking open the valve.

Two burly firemen wrestle with the hose and direct it into the sundry shop next door, and the water power is so intense it immediately breaks the front windows, and scatters all the holiday greeting cards and Scotch tape and red and green decorations and paper airplanes flying from the ceiling, they all get tangled up and blown god knows where.

Then the police officers tell us to "Move back. Move back. Go on. Get back." Then they notice some kids resting on their bicycles and shoo them away.

It's really sad standing there watching these nice old buildings burn down. It's really sad. My first job was at that drug store, dusting shelves, bringing out Kotex, soda jerkin' from time to time when it got busy, stealing hot peanuts out of the lighted peanut rack, then teasing old June Bug, the pretty red-haired fountain girl who was just a bit too mature for me at that time, but who I wished I had dated, now that I look back on it all.

So, shit, the corner drugstore and the sundry shop and the bakery, all went down that early morning, and Phil and I stood there watching, mesmerized.

The cold temperatures just froze up everything near the end. All the water in the streets, all the overhead electric and phone lines, all the walls and windows. Solid ice.

Then it was the firemen's turn to clean up. They put away their hoses and they tried to push the debris out of the way so people might use the sidewalk a little.

Meanwhile I noticed the neighborhood kids just stealing everything they could lay their hands on. I mean jewelry was in the street and books and magazines and all kinds of bottles and cans, some not damaged at all except for being dirty.

And one kid, I think they called him Spunk, Spunk Norris was his full name, but I believe his real first name was Clarence. Anyway, he was right at the sundry window, pulling at a large toy truck, wedged in the debris and frozen solid, frozen to the deck of the window, and he was pulling it, yanking at it with his gloved hands, but he just kept slipping off that damn toy truck. So he threw his gloves down and climbed in the window and pulled as hard as he could. Then a police officer came over and yelled a couple a times, "Stop that. Stop that!"

But old Spunk didn't hear, so the policeman walks over and puts his hand on Spunk's shoulder and shakes him a bit. I heard him say, "That's enough, son. Go home. You've got enough loot for one day."

Spunk looked up sheepishly and shrugged, got down from the window and started to walk back home. He was a good kid. Just got a little greedy.

I walked home too. Phil wanted to stay until all the fire engines left, but I had to get home. I had some loot myself. I had picked up about three pairs of earrings and a bracelet for Jill. I couldn't find anything for myself. But maybe these trinkets would put Jill in a good mood, so I wouldn't have to do too much cleaning at home.

When I opened the front door, Jill was vacuuming upstairs. I hollered up, "It's a really big fire."

She hollered back, "It better be."

***

Part 2 The Peach Page

My interest in writing blossomed at Gesu School
where we were taught by Notre Dame nuns and
some very talented lay teachers as well. The nuns
read to us constantly, sometimes early in the day
or after noon recess. They read entire books to us,
and we all hushed as the next chapter was read.
The school itself worked on our imaginations as
well. Many of us participated in plays in the old
gym. Overlooking us in a large room, the
Women's Club would meet for lunches and
coffees. My urge for coffee spiked each time
they met, for the aroma permeated the entire school.

***

Haunted Leaves on Torrey Hill

smoky jalopies
parked near burning blackened leaves
portray delusion.

A&P Surrealism

murderous waves of melting chocolate bars
seem to attack the spineless dieters
and slurp thick coats of butterscotch
on top of glazed hams nightly,
while farm boys carry barbecue
to secret places.

oh, the poor fat man,
slave to urgings unknown since
cadavers rose from cream sauces
long ago in Mesopotamia
on the River Styx
or some other god-awful
place where curdled goat's milk
had been a delicacy.

now resolute folks flock
to K-Marts buying oatmeal
ice cream and truly
devastating tofu meat patties,
washing said delights into stomachs
clothed with XXX sized nylon,
just enough to hold them in
before diet beer foams in
transformed quagmires,
and gypsy balladeers, singing
tunes by Willie Nelson toking on
fruit lollipops, plop grease
down stuffed shirts.

Christmas Eve: 1954

the dog stood beside the front door
dingling a small bell
and its sound was pleasant
yet no one moved.

we all saw a certain
wickedness in the smile,
long tongue
licking its black lips, its short hair lilting
with each breath it took.

someone put on Handel, hoping
for momentary distraction,
but we still sat on fluffed up
couches staring into cold
dog eyes while it smirked,
ringing the bell
in some odd way, its tail
rampant with messages,
clanging against the door's
hard oak,
slapping a drummer's beat
to provoke us on the holiday
morn, a cold sleet bouncing off
the porch windows,
a pile of icy nuggets
looming to be shoveled away.

Christmas Morning: 1951

most of the bulbs flicker now,
each red and green a glimmer
sent to the world's
children.

ancient events tinsel out
in explosions of color,
red cheeks,
white breath,
eager kids sledding.

our mobile society
lurches toward Bethlehem,
chanting reindeer songs,
searching for meaning.

boxes litter the floor,
one more toy,
one more tie,
one more game
tossed into the void.

Sirens Rise

turn around ten times
and jump the fence.

holy ground here so pace yourself,
avoid the pitfalls,
scratch clay and reveal secrets.

phone home and check,
did the mail deliver
some gory thing?

repeat ten times
"oh god oh"
and lie down.

feel the grass grow
filter out the darkness
in your heart.

crawl slowly if you can
and touch the toes of others
who screech, scrape and hope.

monitor heartbeats
hear the sirens rise.

Two-Car Garage

found it in the refuse bin
out by the dim-bulbed garage.

found it like a surgeon
finds a cancer, blooming
under the skin.

looked up to the moon,
its dark side all aflame,
curse words stamped white.

sent it to momma
who cried, your words
all disconnected.

found time to listen,
recorded your voice
while you drove away.

felt some emotion,
a gargle, a swish
of mouthwash.

spit it out,
but it grew back,
silver vines spinning
black lies.

Sonic Booms

if you hold back an inch,
if you plot disaster,
let me know.

I'll be ready, harpsichord
music hinting old-fashioned
fire, brimstone,
belly-up sharks swirling
down the drain.

let me in, backdoor's locked.
closet's full,
bedroom's bonged off
its foundation.

I can take it,
let me decide and
if you do, then release
my soul; fractured
bones can heal.

Ottawa Tavern Aftermath

momentary intuition a flash
a beam a rat-tat zinger
poised to explode.

plink of olive in a dry
beer light someone sipping
but admiring a blink
a toast to the stage lights.

gulping quickly but not
quickly enough a sad case
of infatuation bloating and big
like a ribbon through
chocolate.

moment to moment a dagger
clinks on cellophane its moisture
splashing tingles
up someone's spine.

but behold the phantom
sluiced with melted marshmallows
licking drops off
concubines.

Along the Tracks

shadows help and shoes
that fit a road map
seldom used flops
danger to hot thoughts.

escaping seems reason-
able but plans flicker
disappear and sex seems
too obvious.

taking the A-train but in a
backseat far from speed
the urge to fly gives way
to the practical.
stoke muffins in pockets
bring yogurt cups cold
from refrigeration and climb
down from the tracks.

instead follow the moon
and while it blooms
touch fingers to sunflowers
wishing for love.

Barbershop Jig

wood burned by sun
scoured by lightning
found in a field
after the fire, Jacob reigns now
propped outside the liquor store
needing to be lacquered but
resisting a polish, the great Indian's
head smiles, a gentle moment,
but customers rub his nose
until he dances,
the perpendicular
flouted by passion
for the dance,
his bear skin
flopping with each jump.

Little Red Wagon

no dosing now,
not on the downward trip
passing by the big bump
and steering with your tongue
rolling it up in a ball,
stretching to reach
your best, watching
bushes, shrubs and mighty ants
rush by while brother Bob
calls out dinner time
and you better get back
or pops will whip
your ass with that giant
celery stalk he keeps
for crispy moments
when kids in wagons
come home late
to supper.

Bank Nite at the Colony

just when it happened seems
impossible to bring up from memories
too deep for fried chicken
too shallow for creamed tuna on toast,
but somewhere something happened
and chairs meant for round bottoms
were crunched by backsides too big
to flop, too big to fit into cinema seats,
where life's deadly degeneration
plunged posteriors into another dimension
and traveling by big wheels seemed not only
correct but largely, hugely appropriate
to a culture that whips potatoes high
and beef jerky snaps before one can
down the rotundly ironic diet coke.

The Cat That Cried Dead Kittens

so sure was I that I rolled the big rocks
away, pushing them deeper into the snow so
I might see. I waited
this night for the moans, the agony of the wild
beast patrolling the backyard each full moon,
a cat like no other mother, not concealing the depth
of sadness, the voice howling with pain,
carrying her dead kittens
though the yard and past the creek,
each step locked in icy snow, no problem to track
the morbid cargo down through thick thistles,
their summer brightness grayed by winds near zero,
the beast raking its belly
in painful petulance, with all her mother's zeal
confounded by hunger, tears and babies
who would not wake even as she kissed
their fur and loved their little toes.

Artie Shaw Summer

hot mustard on hot dogs
the zing of goose liver on rye
a touch of purity
the Artie Shaw recording
and over in the corner,
one lost toy,
captured from flames,
its tires smelling
of fossils off the Dead Sea,
millions of years ago
petroleum was a living thing
like you, like my grand-daughter
now playing a quick game
of croquet,
all jumbled inside,
so excited by warm summer air.

Lunch at Plaskon: 1947

mugs of white lined up
still wet from the dishwasher
tough solid mugs
built to last, carrying
the black easily too,
the factory workers lining up outside
eager for java and clunkers,
turning them into dunkers,
a wisp of black steam
caught in mid-air
by tongues turned mute
the distant grumbles
stifled till noon
when the whistles would blow
their luncheon magic.

The Back Room

sometimes I'd go there after deliveries slowed
and makeshift jobs taunted anger.
sometimes I'd hear the whispers
covered by silence, just one
word or two, an adjustment made,
the couple listening before
building their excitement again.
sometimes I'd be jealous
and tap the door in my
fantasy but status excluded me
and the thin white skirt
would be raised to exposure
by fingers too neatly trimmed
by hands too softly probing.
sometimes in frustration I'd sneak
away waiting for their emergence,
watching them holding hands,
my girl going back to the cash register,
he back to counting pills.

Pond-Crack at Walden

orange fish
probe noses against
cold veneer
plunk noiselessly in their
lethargy, mind-numbing
cold inches down
the solid crystal
bubbles encased
in beauty while pressures
oft created in fuming
nature's grasp
increase by bumps
till the rip of power
cracks across the smooth.

Oak Openings Hummingbirds

too cute for most, invisible in morning
sunshine, the creatures live at a rate
so speedy, their wings flapping
till invisibility becomes a metaphor
for infinity; these thumb-sized creatures
can amaze the way Stravinsky frightens,
motions bleeding into conscience,
high-pitched screams blending with the lawnmowers
of summer, beauty castigated by gasoline-fired noise,
blistering eardrums;
awake and watch!
no video can stop-motion such little
hearts, eager beaks poking flowers
for edible ambrosia, flitting away as if
their minds could brew wine.

Black Clouds at Reno Beach

no shock to see
waves lapping,
wooden docks slapped happy
by filtered green, the blue sky
cloudy, the sun refracting
rainbows in puddles, but briefly;
most people climb onto sailboats,
keels deep in clarity, all prepared
for wind;
the black storm
approaches,
west winds whipping sails, skippers dogging
passengers to hurry, all rain drops big
and blasting splotches on cotton
shirts advertising fun,
with fantasy gambling down the highway,
free lunches for all.

Centennial Jazz

sleepy eyes see jazz, tired ears hear
clouds scudding across
the bay;
surreal noises squeak on glass windows,
and donuts cry out to be
eaten; phantasms rise like mist
from dirty clothing; tomorrow's
tasks frighten the brave;
one last drink to ponder;
let it slip down throats
willing those nightmares to be
gargled till dawn;
friends smile dusty gestures,
no sense noises rise
from pretty mouths,
their lipstick traces
left on cups of cold
coffee, cigarettes lending
dreary smog to night's chill.

Mood Indigo

gloom trapped miracles inside,
for nothing penetrates your fogs:
they come like stale uncles,
teeth rancid with smoke.
soon bits of dreams dissipate,
only frogs' guttural groans
fill the house.
you kiss windows
oozing with dead bugs, your tongue
lolling on glass, licking
decay.

Bargain City Grand Opening

sweeping nostrums induce
moods of optimism,
architects clicking their pencils in notebooks.
their eyes see shafts of steel jutting
from abandoned cemeteries, the native dead
shaking as each pylon
thrusts their heaven
into cold clay.
arising is a trophy
to gluttony, hard rockers blazing
tunes at the grand opening,
customers shuffling across marble floors,
rolling their fat bodies
toward glimmering ghosts,
objects to be placed in wooden cabinets,
waiting for the years to crumble.

Fairmont Pharmacy Fire

When the big fire started in the bakery basement
near the corner of Upton and Bancroft, I was just
getting up from sleep. All the sirens woke us,
and my parents let us go watch the fire.
Fairmont Pharmacy, the sundry store and the
bakery were heavily engulfed. At first, we watched
from a distance, but as the flames were put out,
we got brave. Walking on the slick, icy sidewalk,
we picked up items frozen on the ground. I got
some earrings, other neighbor kids plucked
up toy cars. I went to the broken front window
at the sundry store where a huge, toy, fire truck
was imbedded in ice. I tried to get it out, but
a fireman came over and told me that
"I had enough loot." I returned home with
many trinkets, but sadly did not get that truck.
Only much later did I realize I had been
a common looter, and might have been
shot in more modern times.

Brush-Off at the Art Museum

mystification first, the surface covered with honey,
students grinning while the professor
spreads fluid on lacquered enamel.
creation becomes a joke, laughter blurts
messages, each brush a stroke
for cool design,
their competition for attention
rakes his porous skin, and graduate
students pause, their jealousy a yellow
smoke rising above
the art.

Dad's Pall Malls

destroying his own lungs
seemed a joyous communion;
he'd ask for lights,
bum cigarettes, block
open doorways, spreading soot
in spring air,
inhaling the dust
of death,
and laughing to display
his yellow teeth,
his soul not bothered
by destruction, yet now
attaching
a nicotine patch seems somehow
more polite, rescuing
children from bronchial
attacks, and prolonging
our own lives
for one more sunset,
one more breath,
one more glimpse
of what he
might have been.

Thimbles at the Gallery

a gerrymandered plain stretching
the canvas to forever,
then limbo, no color patterned
after Matisse,
no bright sunflowers
like Van Gogh.
no,
just flattened orchids
like movie sets,
each one artificial
yet more real,
as sewing machines rock
and thimbles scurry
home.

Plastic Desperation

footsteps in the hallway,
a clank of metal,
the small door opening,
then clicked shut.
wait, wait, the footsteps
sound, a rush of cold air,
he's gone.
out like a spider you bolt,
keys unlocking the mystery.
one lone letter,
no magazines today.
inside, a bit of life
for you.
a form letter revealed, your sharp nails
clawing the envelope,
your eyes licking the print
for news.
but no friendship in this,
no warming note of love:
just a notice
to be gone,
the rent
is overdue, and your
plastic doesn't work
on old Mr. Kurtz.

At the Peristyle

the echoed hall,
more lonely than remembered,
no softness remains,
each visitor tortured by boiled dinner's smell,
carrots, potatoes, beef;
they leave through unlocked doors,
while captives wait, sneezing,
and you adjust the volume,
opening your mouth to shout
inked notes
from Ibsen, dark, dank despair;
the audience recoils,
each yawn floating criticism
to style, to nuance, and
you, you,
cough the echoes again
to volumes of unopened pamphlets,
a guest speaker demoted
to impotent dancing bear.

War and Peace

I was assigned "War and Peace"
at St. Francis, a truly awesome book. Just the
heft impressed me. Each of us was required
to write a book report, including extended
character sketches of all major persons.
I think I received a B+, not bad for me,
but that dear priest was the person who
influenced me to become an English teacher.

Libbey Court Ghost

your posed legs limit
choices; each artist lifts sharp pen
to thick paper,
tracing your cleft-tones black,
the white space
giving depth to thoughts
stuck in 1973, the Carpenters
humming lost tunes,
while an annoying facial
tic bruises the moment
purple, and satin dolls harangue
the truth:
to voice pleasure on vinyl,
then die so thin.

Ottawa River Romance

green scum on the creek,
aeration bottled up in tubes
too rich for budgets.
fish die,
belly up white in green muck,
but I can see your eyes
bright and yearning. just
ten long steps across the murk.
if only feet could find
the strong, solid rocks
to plant, the way would clear,
the bouncing, water-logged limbs
would part, the sewer smell would purify,
and your soft hand would guide me home.

Blizzard near St. Anthony's

first, recognize options.
so the snow falls?
so your car resembles
a bump midstream, its snout
a glob of ice cream?
measured in feet, flakes pile on,
the football metaphor a rumbling hush.
step out, hear the calm, only scraping
shovels grate their response
to limbo. lifting your knees completes
your intent, yellow buses huffing while children
plunge into drifts of fluff, the last thing
visible their backpacks of pink.

Reverie

if the song seemed right,
she'd play it again,
the stylus dropped just so,
the speakers rasping the viola;
so we sat longer, the couches
slipping into duress.
soon the tea would appear,
cream cheese cake too,
a bit of ice cream for some.
duty was painful, made bearable,
made somehow fine,
by soft hands, cool fingers,
slipping secrets between helpings
of Mozart and mud pies,
her smile ready with irony
and a pinch of wit.

The Porch on Freeman

most come to visit with a mild static
in their legs, easing off first by the swing, its lilt
evident, its promise of ecstasy
so real to the touch.

only chain keeps you up, its easy screech
of back and forth
interrupted by jasmine blossoms
whiffing perfume on dust mites.

breathe deeply, inhale, your intoxication
sweeps spiders off their perches,
knocks mosquitoes off
their food runs, blotchy skin
still ripe with red blood.

stop at your peril,
push off with toes so happy to be
useful, no insects fly at such low range,
just the perfect evening coolness,
with pink sunset's dancing hopes
alive.

Parade down Madison

castaways leap live wires
catch and drape light gleaming
on green, red, each bead famous
cherished and maddening crowds lurch
as one hand grasping concupiscence
so gluttonous wanting wanting
screaming ancient needs caught up in
crushed lungs bursting for more
wrapping strings around light poles
necks thick with Technicolor tripe
young ladies drunk with envy
produce globules bouncing under shirts
out of shirts bouncing
to be tugged wanting to be
wrapped in tinsel
waiting to be groped.

Downtown Pub Crawl

all aboard buses leaving each seat
filled with raucous cussedness
no beer allowed now dump it out
and shake your booty on board
next stop ten minutes timed
by jesters dressed in handsome hose
floppy hats gentle voices
seek slithery fishnets capturing
music by the note
struggling for Zydeco bastards
free of inhibitions freely
slacking the night away
belching deep-seated frustrations
stuck in doorways no more
just jimmying jazz melting barbecue
quivering with thirst
for the blues.

She Spoke Soup

most recipes allow
deviance a pinch of pepper
or a cut sausage sprinkled
in gruel offering the guest
a taste of paradise
and old Mrs. Timkins knew soup
knew how it could bind neighbor to neighbor
could leave the taste of memory in your bowl
and on your tongue.
she didn't look for wisdom
and she despised arrogance, instead
opting for kitchen friendships
with young ladies making
homes for fathers too busy
to notice a pale cheek,
a lonely tear at noon.

Before Tiedke's Burned

getcha some fine morning on a
Saturday work begun in earnest
effort maybe a bit of carpentry
on tree choppin' perhaps a window
needin' some flashing
on a back door shimmed too loose, too tight,
too much cold air pushing under doorways,
but the moment
looked for the needed implement
comes up missin' and only the shop
down Summit Street offers
hope if it'll take a dollar or two for some steel
whirligig or hammer to make
the day all pleasant again.

Colony Matinee: 1953

fifteen minutes till curtain,
the lost art of sweeping velvet to the side,
while first flickers of film
shock the sleepy visitors
to war at the front;
serial moments follow
with depth of cars crashing
over precipices, and ladies,
needing closure,
smell the popcorn,
and push rumps past faces
intent on fantasy,
each eye
glazed with butter.

A Free Man

I also liked the name of our street: Freeman,
FREE MAN. "I am a free man," I'd say to myself.
I was completely free and courageous, I thought.
The name was very symbolic, and it fit in with
some of the films of the 1950s we all saw at the
Colony Theater: "The Three Musketeers"
was a big one. When it came out, the whole
neighborhood of kids found swords made out
of small tree limbs, stripped off the bark, and
made weapons. We never hurt each other,
but we staged many sword fights. Dying,
of course, was a practiced art form.

Caboose Yellow at the Lion's Store

sort of a fog today,
the streets glistening with the tactile,
and children's voices monstrously rolling
through alleys covered
with broken whirligigs.
wide windows display miniatures,
playtime colors bounce mist droplets,
coloring panes with frivolous white;
noses poke droplets to the side,
lips speaking lustful thoughts,
press windows,
urging tongues to lick
away thin layers of moisture
to find relief in plastic towns
and locomotives straining up hills,
cabooses yellow in twilight.

Cherry Street Love

once, black licorice teeth
could amuse;
once, cheeks smeared
with coal dust might
resist touch of Dickens
and repel thoughts of church mice
tattling on cats, pink tongues
circling red mouths to kill;
once, each piece of flannel rubbed
necks just so,
with warm
collars sweeping skin,
frigid from winter's blast;
once, night arrived
suddenly,
like a shuttered cage, lopping off
sunshine till morning's bouquet;
once, neighbors grilling
tomatoes for breakfast
forgot to close their door,
and jellied yams
sank beneath swirling gutter streams
heading toward the harbor;
once, you loved me,
and I loved you.

Auction on Junction

after, crowds swayed, parted with money,
sent scattered hopes home for nurturing.
and we were left with tables,
no one else bidding
for oak's heft, most craving the lightness
of futons made in Italy;
sitting there, harrumphing our pleasure,
we lifted and leaned wood against the truck,
checking undercarriages for gum's remains,
chipping away at Blackjack and Tutti-Frutti,
nudging Fleer's Double-Bubble
to oblivion. but best were the carvings
of love, table-tops not marred by ugly
grotesques, but stealth proven honorable,
each stroke a heart, each name
faithful: John hearts Mary,
Juicy loves Crumpet;
those love affairs
from 1946 so real,
their obituaries
never registered the staleness of
Doublemint.

To Waterville

we cut our own this year,
revving up the pick-up,
slamming its doors on the cold.

our own feet warm,
as we move along
stagnant highways for thirty miles,
rocketing down the asphalt,
spotting young deer ready
to cross the road.

a sylvan scene at last,
decorous greenery arranged
in long rows, their branches
fully laden with snow.

we are given an ax,
heavy on our shoulders,
and we march down
the tree lines, looking
for perfection.

taking turns,
we chop, capturing
green life's essence,
leaving a two-foot stub
sticking out, draining sap
to yellow grass,

where next year another
will sprout its readiness
for sacrifice.

After Reading the Peach Page

mother was a silly creature,
testing our senses each day,
but providing a menu,
as we sat stiffly waiting
for dad to finish his newspaper.

we had our own printed message,
concocted by mother as she
basted the turkey,
finding time for notes
of humorous lore
between soups and salads,
ancient rhymes used
fragrantly, freshly pasted
next to knives and forks.

we mustn't touch
till dad sits down, ordering his mashed
potatoes from his own paper list,
a special love note
specifying
portion sizes
and whether we can
have carrots,
and when he'll get a kiss.

Angels at Toledo Hospital

the sterile air holds
mischief for magic births
the slip of molecules shush
the watchers, each a warm
oasis in the fermentation,
while doctors urge
patience the midnight
hour climbs to vertical
and babies anxious
for the light
gasp air
and scream
held proudly
by their ankles
they let mother know
how life excites.

Club Cherry

motion is all,
the dress must be
thin, the weather warm,
the time of day
nearing the edge of insanity.

men gather,
their
bellies held tightly,
waiting for the wink,
the daring flame inside
licking at their
patience.

only one delights
in delay, the endless
dance circling his libido,
his own lips almost tasting
the bare skin, and
lusting for midnight.

Lipstick Smear Gallery

motionless, you cooperated
as I looked through your little
blue purse, picking out your
color: flame pink, a neon
glow; you hesitated
but complied,
taking off your clothing
as I watched.

the line I drew
seemed smooth, a naked
blush blooming on your chest,
my fingers tracing your curves
from toes, up thighs
to that little cleft
near your neck.

bright red rouge thumping,
electricity pumping,
a beat bouncing
between bare breasts.

The Personals

just a few words
flung to the heavens
just an emotion
sent to a friend.

mistake sent a-trembling
lost for an instant
shouldn't have sent it
regret not an option.

if she receives it
it's over for me
new issues selected
my blunder… and how.

wonderful creatures
damned by the phone
hurried up feelings
galactic concussion.

Pulse

awash in rain,
our cars slow down,
stopping at intersections
till babies crawl across,
staying between the white lines,
all the while our feet
pulsate on gas pedals,
anxious to push
on to the pharmacy
where white-clothed graduates
count pills into brown flasks,
slap labels
with our names,
in ink,
in essence we become
junkies waiting for laxatives
and pin-up girls,
promised by scientists
sprightly smiling
knowing what we'll
be doing that night.

Thoughts during Lent

we are left with cold concrete
and we note all ten,
etched by magic,
ten scripted demands
from our invisible god
who dare not show his face;
he wants to be alone
to count
our indiscretions.
his list simple:
just ten items
we might read and obey;
but while he counts
in some ethereal oasis,
we struggle with passion,
and kiss our mother's lips,
kicking our father's shins
and wanting more.

Mistletoe at Ma's

why is it Eddie always
brings good cheer, setting liquor
on the counter, tossing roasted chestnuts
on the record player, and Nat
the King of Cole silently
spins his nostalgic tale
while grandma sips
yellow liquid bursting
with calories and cousins
kiss beneath green twigs
relishing in mistletoe's
subtle sin.

Gesu Midnight Mass

feet frozen by slush
slither to aisle seats near the back
and the awesome cheer of children's
voices echoes high above the chancel
beams, wood and strength medieval
attach to glass windows made bold
by saints and crowned heads, pastel
angels nearly invisible
smile and breathe on necks of altar
boys reciting Latin words of praise,
events exciting in their
history boom loud organ notes,
the pulse of birth reborn
each year at midnight
the hour of memories, devotion
and glory in the child.

Gesu Recess

handling candy as we do,
having it lined up
on conveyors, sliding slowly,
inevitably, our
eyes adjusted to each piece,
each flaw noticed,
like they were
kids we pulled
from line as they
waited for recess:
a mousy brown?
pull it.
a sneezing chocolate-cherry?
stop it.
some foreign piece of hair
out of place
on warm chocolate?
yank it.
the white boxes
shut
till delivery,
warmth
creeping through
the cardboard.
wonder who will
come out and play
today?

Purple Gang Visitation

one vantage takes
time to understand.
the wind wild,
the snow packed
against brick, red
with desire.
magic potions tremble
in beakers.
if these liquids
could flow,
the wind's crystals
might serrate, slash,
might blast Toledo's
neat history, replace it
with scenes from factories,
their brick-red hints
of pain crashed against
spiffy Cadillacs double-parked
outside meat markets,
waiting for that slice
of sirloin wrapped
in white paper,
the beast's blood
oozing through,
onto luxury,
fifties tail-fins flashing away
to deep, dark recessed
garages, footmen
ready to open

the kitchen door,
madmen stepping out
into the frost.

Woodlawn Cemetery

families tied in knots,
administrators type,
the old machines clank,
the cause of death easy:
"malnutrition
mal-treatment
grande or petite mal."
strange how parents
feel, their adult children
should be put down like sick ponies,
each cold-skin-form placed in wooden
boxes, carted to the fields.
but regulations require
identification, process,
each form lifeless,
no complaints,
but agencies demand
decorum.
and parents want more:
erasure,
oblivion,
their god-awful child
a constant slap,
an insane departure
from DNA so preciously escaped,
yet genealogy won't
be fooled by graves
numbered, not named.
someone searching the years

will see connections
to type's mind-warped blackness.

Tree Lot on Alexis

suffering from anorexia
(too little Miracle-grow consumed)
a rock-hard home
(up in the hills)
a long ride back
to the comfort
of family
some greenery for the season
(a bit of frenzied shopping)
followed by music
those notes medieval
harmonize with tinsel
scraps from aunt's old
tree (a jumble
of thoughts)
for such
little boughs
almost an after-thought
the tea and Christmas
cookies rolled up
(on the plate)
for you and me.

Perrysburg I-Hop Crush

old thought patterns
confusing me most of that day,
the day after you left,
a confusing time,
filled with croissants,
blackberry wine
and maudlin memories,
like syrupy fruit
clinging to electrical
impulses
down my spine,
a sort of enervation,
a power loss in my soul,
when drunken beauty lurching
out from the subconscious
took the place of real
women singing songs of desire.

Smooth Jazz—ooks!

a short, spastic article
in today's news
spurted indecent, ineluctable
horror.
that FM radio
dial has lost
its charm,
its melodic imagery
the cool jazz station's signal
snapped off, replaced
by country station
number five-hundred-and-thirty-three,
not that twanging is wrong
or decrepit
or damned,
but too
much twang
becomes gol'dang
and even Shania
can go hang.

Rocky's on Telegraph

once children lose themselves
near displays
parents blurt messages
to heartfelt needs.
total damage
rises,
stillness broken by tiny
footsteps on linoleum,
and old-fashioned shapes
once dynamic and needed
assume the slope of shards
on concrete.
impeded by signs
adults tiptoe
lest earthquakes rattle,
and "break it, buy it,"
trembles nerves,
one kid captured,
another still running
down aisles
slippery with crystals.

East Harbor Cellulite

turning so slowly
in front of mirrors,
miniscule motions
terrify.
bodies resist deployment
mostly, though forcing
thighs to grind gingerly
exposing flaws
marbleizing into age
(a moment of horror).
flesh procures moments
of self-destruction.,
even self-hatred,
not stopped by willpower
entirely,
but beach towels might help
as hot-toed march
to ocean begins.
not jiggling seems
to help poised, swollen breasts,
yet legs reveal
decrepitude, ineptitude,
those invisible eyes
of strangers
not impressed.

Ten Mile Creek

a deeper brown haunts
the well of understanding,
some broken tube
or filter within the bowels,
the intestines plotted
beneath our streets supposed
to bring us the cold and delicious,
the cool liquid heated
to float rubber duckies
in daughters' bathtubs,
the hot liquid cooled
to quench fires raging
when mothers attack,
their disappointments
finally too hot
to stop,
their hands weapons
to crash and splinter
forgotten desires
for cold, rushing water
shushing them
to heaven
down streams
and into whirlpools.

Cold Fingers

your visit, that cold, cold night,
you ran your fingers along my hair
and disrobed,
looking for love;
and I
replied in whispers,
avoiding hurt feelings,
yours and mine.
I had hoped for something
else, but your soft body
radiated heat.
you seemed possessed,
my wants so obvious,
and I felt
your nails
slide along my spine,
tracing your way
home.

The Silk Robe

Waking each morning,
I could hear you downstairs,
fixing that first mild cup,
your quiet step mindful
of Saturday morning,
lawnmowers not grumpy yet,
the neighbors respecting
the last warm days.
Out on the porch I'd find you,
settled in with peanut butter toast,
a wan look on your pretty face,
the leaves of fall
whispering by the screened
porch, your foot pushing against the floor
to move the swing,
yellow, gold, red,
autumn colors
matching your silk robe.

Ducks at Crane Creek

Stillness on the morning pond,
no boats slipping through cool-clear.
Geese off somewhere,
flying behind home-made airships,
going south, going south.
Weather changes quickly,
a hint of dark clouds, a shift of wind;
the placid waters shiver and move,
snippets of a wave, then three, seven,
splashing in secret
next to the bank
where we had found
duck eggs
in early summer.
We wrap our coats quickly, sink
our hands deep into pockets.
North wind lifts up collars,
shakes us deeply,
but we walk on anyway,
moving toward snow.

Going to War

You talk of servicing me,
as if some mechanism
must be fixed
or straightened out.
I try to talk of love
or devotion, yet your eyes wander
towards other men, other toys,
some politely bowing to you,
as they pass our table.
Asking for service seems
too bold, too much like
requesting the waitress.
Will she find
the time?
Will she have other
customers to serve?
Servicing me seems as if I
should leave you a tip
for noble gestures.
Is that what you
want? Is that your
need? Will your hands
grasp me tonight,
squeezing for cash
until I sigh?

Jerry Springer Visits the Mall

When they married,
she was sixteen
and flirtatious. She'd hug him
in the bathroom as he
shaved, her hands working down
to his pajamaed hips, then a light
caress on his open front, her
fingers searching inside,
for bared hard flesh,
her mocking laugh a tease.
He complained.

"Control your daughter,"
he said. She smiled. "She's just
a teenager," she said. "She
has her boy friends. You can meet them."

Yes, he met them on the couch,
after midnight. She often sent him
downstairs. "Check up
on them," she said.
And more than once
he sent them running
butt-naked
into the frosty wind.

Her daughter smiled,
picked up her clothes,
and went to bed.

But those nights when she was
college age,
books littering her room,
she left her
door open, and invited
him inside. Those closed-door studies
they did, he might regret. But the love
she gave, was never
duplicated.
Now that he's gone,
Doesn't the wife wonder why?

Red Wells Opus No. 35

click, click,
click, click,
he had done it once more,
a forgetfulness bound in glory
yet heard,
click, click,
the electric hum,
the clicking of needle in groove,
the empty sound now
of mind in limbo,
remembering
only to put out cigarettes
once too often
left on table tops,
the burn marks a warning,
the music gone
but tell-tale
vinyl clicks reveal
a sadness
as age destroys
living tissue
and the memories
linger
only in eclectic
energy.

Cocoons in Side-Cut Park

moist wings flutter
cocoons burst asunder.
flighty journeys
stumble.
rooftops blaze with thunder.
lightning stifles
softness.
winds plunge
vicious blackness.
the call of plunder
welcomes jays to tear flesh
with hunger.

Ottawa Park Amphitheater

wide expanse of forest,
opening in a natural
amphitheater,
sloped toward the evening sun,
steep down, hazardous,
but Camille agreed,
her fragile body
carefully climbing.
the site was precious,
an enabler for the sound
we hoped could be produced.
instant response from all,
the yellows
the muted blues, the forest greens,
a spot for music.
the audience perched neatly
on mounds of verdant grass,
the orchestra gliding in,
applause polite yet building
to crescendos,
and the piano center stage
like a big black beast,
its nobility heard
while people hushed.
the Shearing sound
portrayed their lives,
their living memories
of class, of civilization,
and brilliancy proclaimed again

that music still thrummed
in hearts so dear.

Locust Song at the Zoo

deep dark house,
but bright moments came
then went,
while each slide
processed the past,
moment at the zoo framed
by simple silhouettes
in autumn cages,
you bunched up
in clean laundry
by the kitchen sink,
ice cream dripping
down your chin,
me laughing while
sparks shot from sparklers
at the Springsteen concert
blinding us in the flash of cameras,
last frame plunking us both
down near the lake,
pink-orange sunset
fading,
our arms twined around each
other, the memory
of locusts
haunting warm moist air,
one year
before the final, sudden split.

Sculpture at the Glass Pavilion

each head is disguised.
but we slide down museum
corridors anyway, no alarms sounding,
no silent sentries touched.

eerie light captures sculptures' shine
head reflections bouncing off protective plastics,.
our own flesh-orbs use eyeball's glint
for information, gathering
impressions of noses, cracked skulls,
fire-hot crevices
the artist had patiently embedded.

night adds aura, dignity
to clay.
shafts of green splash like lime juice
against cold faces, beheaded monsters,
frigid flesh immortalized grotesquely.

human face to clay face,
nomenclature thrusts
life into death.

Night Antics

you hadn't slept
at all
you were tossing
hints
tempting me
but your
antics to win
seemed
like steel revolvers
seen through
lace
wanting what you
wanted
testing
and rejecting
while my own
urgings
stumbled, faltered,
your mood so damn
provoking yet
your lips lying
while they kissed

Bins of Beauty at Boogie

before the plastic,
the brittle cases closing
music in,
the bins held classic
style, artwork ennobled
by caring artists' hands
on backgrounds telling stories.
the gentle liner notes
revealed substance,
lyrics sung by voices
scented in truth.
one can feel the style
the care of production,
with vinyl sleeved inside
carefully, so luminous
in soft light
and opened with delight,
played on turntables
whirring quietly,
with morning light
quieting conversation's
respectful awakening.

Snap

flannel cloth awaits,
fire flickers, snapping, snap, pop,
raging fire's rapture.

***

"B" Movie Review

I get a real crappy feeling each time I have to meet a girl somewhere. Don't ask me why. I just feel crappy. Like why don't I just stop over to her house and we can walk over to the Auburndale Grill, sit down and share our repast of grilled cheese, pickles and potato chips with our coffee? Why not?

Regardless, Fridays are not really special anyway, I was telling Jayne, my girlfriend of these last four weeks, Fridays are for the guys to go out, for god's sake. Not no time to have a date. And there's no good movie on at the Rialto anyway, just some 'B' film we saw last week, starring Dana Andrews, some crime drama that's not too bad, but who wants to see it again?

These gray Fridays in February are even worse, like today, I told myself as I shuffled down Milburn Avenue, scraping up some of last years leaves still frozen to the pavement.

Jayne lived on the other side of Auburn, so it made sense to her that I could walk half way, and we'd both end up in the same place at half the time. She was lookin' out for me, she said. Savin' me from gettin' too tired so I can sit up awake all through the movie and not fall asleep like, I must admit, I sometimes do, especially if the movie has Dana Andrews in it. What kinda name is Dana for a guy anyway?

I was early, so I took my time, trying to notice the beauty of nature, like Jayne tells me to do, but I can't see no beauty since it's getting dark like it usually does at 6 p.m. I thought I'd just go over across the street on

Auburn and roll a few games at Gazzolo's Bowling Alley, and see if Mick and Dennis were workin'. Mick sets pins most of the week for fifty cents an hour, getting to bowl free whenever it's not too busy and, of course, Dennis just hangs out there and shoots the shit with anyone until it's time to go drinkin' with the guys. Like I say, Fridays should be for drinkin', none of this "let's have dinner at eight and don't be late," then see the ten p.m. movie.

But I don't know why I'm complaining. Jayne puts out at the movie, and the back row always seems good enough for me no matter what movie is on or what tremendous times friends are havin', getting drunk and singing songs over at Kurt's Cafe.

Anyway, tonight is somethin' special, Jayne says. And she's got a surprise for me. She's been kinda mad at me for forgetting her birthday last week, and she says I'll learn my lesson sometime. But she's sweet and I told her I was sorry, so what's the big deal?

So I open the big front door of Gazzolo's and the gentle, wafting breeze hits me with smoke and the smell of beer. I wander over to the shoe check-in and I see that Stevie's workin' tonight. Stevie's a funny name for a girl, but it's short for Stephanie or something so she doesn't mind when we shorten it and call out, "Stevie, I need a size eleven," which is my shoe size even though I'm just 5'8" soakin' wet. And don't give me no shit about having big feet. They make me more stable in the wind, I tell everybody, so just clam down.

Anyway, I get the shoes from Stevie and sit down behind alley number five, my favorite number and my all time favorite alley because I can just get in the groove so fast. I mean, the ball I throw fits this alley, and I'm not talking about the actual ball, cuz sometimes I can't find good old number 289, and the bowling ball I usually try to find. Shit, even with ball 211 or 239 I can hit this alley. My high score being a 759 series, you can see what I mean. I love alley number five.

So, I'm puttin' on my shoes and looking around for Dennis at the same time. He ain't here, which is odd. I notice someone waving and hollering at me from alley number ten, so I wave back.

"How they hangin', Mick?" I shout and he laughs and says, "Eat shit," which I find partially amusing. But now I feel ready and it's just six-fifteen so I figure I can roll a three gamer, freshen up a bit in the john afterwards and still make it on time to dinner with Jayne.

Mick's off duty for awhile so he and I issue one of our regular challenges, which means whoever loses buys the winner a beer next Friday night, seeing as how I'm not goin' anywhere tonight.

So, Mick goes first and wipeouts in the right gutter on his first official roll, cause he has this big hook, that if he don't hit the right board real close to the gutter, the damn ball gets no traction and sort of just fades into the gutter. On his next throw he's lookin' at ten pins again and he's getting' pissed already. That's a good sign cause when Mick's pissed, he's no good. He picks up an eight total for the first frame and the rest of the evening I keep going spare, spare, spare, strike, spare, spare, and battle to around a 180 game each time.

But old Mick is just plain bad. His high game is 129, and his famous hook is laid up in the hospital with terminal gutteritis. I couldn't help laughing at him a bit, but not too much cause we all get bad days.

Then I notice that it's seven-forty-five and time to wash the armpits a little after I turn in my shoes. I ask Stevie if she's seen Dennis at all, and she says, "No, it's not like him to miss a Friday."

I agree but have little time to chitchat. Now I gotta drive over to the Auburndale Grill, meet Jayne and go see Dana Andrews again. Shit, I hoped Jayne's in a lovin' mood or that movie could be deadly.

It's two blocks to the Auburndale Grill and my armpits are still wet a little, and the sweat from bowling is making me chilled. It must be that my underpants are wet with sweat too, cuz the wind is almost making me shiver.

At first when I look through the front window of the grill, I can't see nothin' for all of the steam on the windows. I walk in past the Wurlitzer, Johnny Ray is singing that dumb song, "Cry," and I see Dennis just walking back from the restroom, so I yell out, "Hey, Dennis! We missed you over at Gazzolo's. Where were ya?"

But he just keeps movin' away from me toward the corner booth, my corner booth, where I take most of my women friends so we can have some privacy. *Shit*, I think, *Dennis has some woman back there and he's in my booth.*

So I amble over, casual-like, to stick a needle in old Dennis because of him having a date and missing out on his usual Friday night drunk, but the girl with him stops me dead. All I can see is her long, blonde hair and that fluffy, pink cashmere sweater but I know it's Jayne. So what the shit is Dennis doin' sittin' with her? I'd like to know.

So I take two steps more and lean over the booth

with my two hands on the table and say, "What the shit is up?"

Then, Jayne screams, "Surprise!" and I know now what happens when you forget some girl's birthday.

I also know when I'm beat so I just salute them both with my middle finger and decide to drive back over to Gazzolo's. Maybe Mick can get off early so we can grab a few beers. After all, it's Friday night.

***

Part 3 Opinion Page

A golfing family lived in a house
next to our duplex on Freeman. Our side yards touched,
so we spent much time there playing games.
My dad taught us many games.
One was called "nigger baby," a very
horrible name but one we gave little
thought to as kids. Later, I was appalled by
the racism involved in the game.
Each kid would dig a small hole, large
enough for a tennis ball to roll into.
One kid was it, and rolled the ball
down the line of holes. Each of us had
one of our feet next to our hole.
As soon as the ball was rolled, everyone
took off running, except for the kid who
owned the hole where the ball stopped.
That kid would slam his foot down on the
ball and yell, "Stop." Everyone had to
freeze and not move. Then the kid with
the ball would throw it at the nearest person.
If he hit you, you received a very small
stick to place in your hole. The stick was
a "nigger baby" and you were then "it" and
had to roll the ball. Whoever got three
nigger babies first would be out. It went
that way until there was just one player left.
The symbolism of this game touches
upon many of the white prejudices
against blacks: having babies out of

wedlock, receiving welfare, driving
around in Cadillacs. All these canards
were lingering over this childhood game,
teaching us prejudice.

***

Cold Times

Two weeks before the coal man was to deliver and the bin was almost empty. Sure, Frank figured, he could order an emergency load, but where would the fifteen bucks come from, not from Beth. She was out of work now that the holidays were over and no one else seemed to need a part-time cashier.

Then there was the rumor of a strike vote over at the plant. Frank was sure that a strike should have been done before Christmas, thereby putting more pressure on management right before the busy season. But no, the union stewards all voted for after the holidays. They didn't want to miss any payroll checks before Christmas shopping was done. And they figured that the plant had stockpiled enough plastic powder for Christmas and beyond, so the only way to hurt the company was to strike after the holidays.

It sort of made sense, but now the strike talk was even stronger and Frank could barely pay for rent, insurance, food and furniture payments while working full time. And with Beth being off work and pregnant, he didn't really know which way to go, but he had begun looking for another job, at least part-time for now.

On this Tuesday morning, Frank groggily woke up, washed his face and hands, sat down with some black coffee and waited while Beth fried up some eggs. He had about thirty minutes before he left for the factory, so he tried to get focused. Beth was beginning to get bigger around the middle and he took pleasure from the realness of having a child.

"Hon, you know I'm real happy were gonna have this kid. It makes me smile, you know, like looking into the future and seeing us with kids and it's spring and we're walkin' through the park."

"Yeah, well, just don't start, Frank. I'm in no mood. You know I didn't want this kid, we can't afford it, and your screwin' around at the wrong time brought us this mess. So, don't think you can talk me into liking it."

Frank immediately frowned, his dream collapsed, and he began to nervously pick on the scab left on his thumb after scalding himself on the coffee pot the previous night. Beth finished the eggs and bacon and plunked them in front of her husband. She busied herself with making her breakfast and put two slices of bread into the toaster for Frank.

The kitchen remained too quiet for comfort, and Frank ate in silence. Beth sat down and began to chew loudly, her lips open, the food visible inside. She had a bad cold and could only breathe through her mouth. Not a pleasant sight for Frank who suddenly got up.

"Gotta go. See you after work." He gave her a kiss on the top of her head, swung a sweater over his shoulder and went outside to start the Nash.

Beth remained at her seat, giving Frank only a slight smile as he left, her thoughts whirring around inside her, thoughts that mostly were egocentric and depressing. Never the gabby sort, when she talked only gloom and predictions of failure came out. Frank was not just beginning to tire of her. His only commitment to her was through the child yet to be born. Who would want to stay around someone who never said nothin' was the way Frank thought about Beth.

In the Nash, Frank backed out to the street, lit a cigarette and started the ten minute drive to the factory.

The lot was filled with the early ones, the hot shots and the ones who lived to work. Frank was none of these. Yes, he worked hard but didn't take pride in loading different dyes into vats, preparing the solutions, carrying supplies, or keeping the machines well ordered. It was a factory job, for chrissakes, Frank would say, and it was a dead end. You worked twenty-five years, retired and got a Gruin watch. Big deal. His real life was in his mind and in his new child. There was the future. There was the reason why he worked.

Frank noticed as he parked his car near the far west fence that most of the day shift was still outside, surrounding a speaker who was standing on top of a pickup truck. Locking his doors, Frank then turned and sprinted the hundred or so yards to the factory entrance to make sure he did not miss the news.

". . . no fair way to do it. There is just no way we can let you down by accepting this contract offer. There are many take backs by management, too many to accept. Real loopholes are placed in your retirement plan, and the payout you must give for medical is up 100%. It is a contract that we cannot support."

The speaker was the Local 725 AFL/CIO union leader, Jake Karnes, and Jake was vehement. "We cannot allow this contract to pass. We must vote it down even if it means they lock us out tomorrow."

Frank found Marcus Fowler, his friend and co-worker who worked alongside him most of the day.

"What's up, Marcus? Sounds bad."

"Hey, Frank. Yeah, it is bad. The plant is angry at

us and they think they have enough product stockpiled to beat us. But there's no way out. This contract stinks."

"Well, are we working today?"

"Don't know yet. It's up to management."

The eight a.m. whistle blew and streams of men from inside gathered around the union leader, asking questions, listening for answers.

Then the large doors slammed shut. Locks were turned and screwed into place. And the plant closed down. The unit's foreman, a real rat by the name of Tim French, came out and posted a sign.

Men. No work today. You are locked out.

Vote for the Contract and return.

No questions asked.

"Management CARBIDE PLASTICS"

The union members were astounded. They had been outflanked. The plant was closed and no vote had even been taken. It was a blatant power move by a company that was arrogant and mean-spirited. Frank and Marcus walked to their cars, jabbering like crazy. Word was out concerning a union meeting at the Arena that night at eight to discuss strategy. Both Frank and Marcus agreed to show up.

At home that evening, Beth refused to listen.

"Listen, asshole. You got me pregnant, now you and your hothead union buddies have got you out of a good job. It's your fault, you fool. If you don't work, I'm out of here."

"Beth, sweetheart. We can work this out. It's not my fuckin' fault. We were locked out. The plant locked us out."

"Yeah, sure, Frank. Sure. Make excuses. You know that there was gonna be a strike. Don't try to kid me. You wanted a strike. You're so fuckin' lazy, you ought to be out of work."

Beth's temper heated the cold apartment air. Frank stared at Beth in amazement. He took her at first for a strong woman, a woman who would stand by her man. He had been wrong before about her, and now it was all too obvious. She liked to blame others, even her man when times got hard.

The picket line the next day was extremely cold, even for February. It was ten degrees when Frank showed up for his first day of picketing. The soup kitchens were there, the strike placards were everywhere, and Frank and his union buddies were strong. They were gonna hold out until summer if they had to.

But one by one the men talked about their women at home, bitching about the strike, complaining about the lack of money, complaining about their cold homes.

If the union lost the battle, it wouldn't be their fault or the company's fault.

All the men agreed. Their women might let them down again.

Security Moms

panel discussions and focus groups
reveal phenom moms made famous by classic
motivations: fear, a fulsome fuzz of patronizing
politics, each mom secure in her family,
but mall shopping so important: five kids lost in the hot
    sun
while moms parked baking Lexus wheels
near the Guess shop, factory-splotched jeans
calling to spandex,
moms lock doors,
crack windows, fearing only
terrorist threats to bomb
their food courts, the kids forgotten
in blurs of yellow, pink,
and powder blue fabric as moms shop
till their kids drop,
yet they talk-talk-talk
security from weird perspectives,
distant evil men planting bombs
in malls, Baskin-Robbins exploding
in cherry nougat ecstasy.

Say Your Prayers

Baghdad reeks,
the stench of phosphorous,
the lightly-tinged patina
of yellow on the balconies
in the green zone.

Safe from evil, troops swim
in Saddam's pool, bask
on porches while distant rockets
flicker flames of dread.

But safety's relative nature
urges caution; men say their
prayers before bedtime,
and arcing, luminous spheres
haunt their dreams
while computers clack messages
to family, friends,
and to the children
they've never seen.

trapped in the green
zone, troops feel a strange suburban life
for a moment,
for a tragedy,
for a misplaced honor,
and they feel nothing like
the heroes they
were meant to be.

Toledo Grid

noble architects settled by chance
deciding in their own mild
mannered way to protect and keep citizens tied
to commerce and unable to escape
the eyes of a community
longing to catch you at
whatever piece of sin you were about
so the streets resembled bars on a cell
each one linked to the next
by cement and sidewalks
each of your attempts
to leave blocked by churches on each
corner every effort to struggle
with the devil blighted by the eyes
of Mrs. Brown head librarian
and chief organ player
at the Methodist Church
where she plodded up the aisle
plotting your demise, god rest your
friggin' soul.

Welfare Department

My mother was a real battler and
a hard-core Democrat.
After she had us three kids, she went
back to work for the Lucas County Welfare
Department. She was a case worker and visited
homes every afternoon to see if the people
qualified for welfare payments. She got
very close to some of these people. Some
gave her vegetables, fruit, in appreciation.
She took her lunch breaks at home so she
could fix us our lunch. At Gesu School
on Parkside, we were allowed to go home
for lunch. We watched Soupy Sales on a
Detroit station and ate bologna sandwiches
with tomato soup before we'd walk back
to school. I loved the names of the streets
in Detroit: Gratiot, Livernois.

Right-Wing Education

so proud, the lawmaker,
strutting his hatred, the microphone
ready to spew venom; nothing
more important than to bash
others, his own DNA so hetero,
and his tongue
so wet with spit.

after his vote he preens,
his long tongue split
and forking, "Now," he says,
"now that we've lynched
the gays and lesbos, now, now,
it's time to talk about kids,"
as if his hate crime didn't
tell kids all
about his oh-so-holy spittle,
as his crucified god
cries in shame.

Scapegoats for Right-Wing Wrath

oh the lives we've ruined,
never looking for our own flaws,
but delving in neighbors'
garbage, holding up
evidence in the courts,
and turning TV's electrical impulses
into gossip, lingering over
details of hypocrisy, waiting for
death penalties
to be posed, audiences
shrieking for blood
poised outside courthouses,
wanting one look,
just one,
of the killer and his chains,
wanting just one rock
to throw,
one knife
to plunge.

Horror

more than the Taliban,
we turn our hate
to picket fences
and lullabies:
talk show hosts
hurl hate speech,
interrupting their own
fathers and mothers;
each is perplexed, angered
by ideas, enjoying put-downs,
insults, one-liners,
spewing hate,
calling names and using
Nazis,
communists,
and terrorists as labels;
flagellating
neighbors,
loved ones,
and daffodils,
as all too yellow
for war.

Disdain for Hollywood

so what if creative brains
are liberal? so what if
needed terrains are invisible?
these creations outmode most
military minds, those
sulking in propaganda,
hating certain differences
and theories, testing their own
but lacking ingenuity; call out
creativity; let them work
on killing; big screens allow magic,
but politics equates dissent with
disobedience; not so, when
intelligence can be tested,
and grunt work can be left
to those who hate.

Why Peter Slept

few decent reasons come to mind,
if your savior prayed for release
from a contract promising
death and you decided to nap,
when all he ever wanted
was some company as he
prayed to the father
to release him
from horrible human
annihilation and angels gathered to chase
away the storm clouds with their wings,
and you slept,
you slept,
you slept away the night.

A Jack Dempsey Moment

spasms control thoughts
one arm lifts then drops
inside thoughts turn
inward even more
those unconscious beings
travel down legs
embedded in soil
a quicksand moment
when dozens of kangaroos hop
and camels ride
with humps swaying;
standing becomes a wobbly blur
and friendly faces
warp with each move.
empty your pockets
for the poor
while weak-kneed muscles
collapse in pain.
have eyeglasses been lost?
will terror trains
rumble in eardrums?
positions taken
in backyards
bring grassy boulders
into view,
large ants crawl
on eyeballs
and blinking takes
so much effort
why try?

Blind and Narrow

some cling to theories
found in old books,
odd and incoherent;
they look for signs of god
in old pizzas, on the bark
of trees, sometimes struggling
for miles looking
for miracles on window fog;
too bad the BB gun
shatters their dreams,
as they search the sand
for hidden meanings,
hidden faces of god,
neglecting the love
they could show
to trees to kids to life.

Neocons

entire limbs cracked off
leaving gaping holes
in TV screens; those
placed nearby suffered
greatly, loss of picture,
sound, a certain ambient disdain
for creatures in the wild.

fractured streets gave way
to huge clumps of oil-based
paint, swept down
from mountain tops, cascading
tumultuously out of hearing
range of those
who sought refuge on top
of the huge, blown-up rubber
Santa Clauses set out
by gas stations to lure
motorists with fruit cake
on their breath.

meanwhile, the last wave
concocted by automated
hot tubs set off
reactions in various wired
politicians
who scanned
their computers for answers
to the question "why?"

then plunging breath mints
into oral cavities, hoping
to please the gods.

After the Election

big city folk can ignore
better than most autistic
kids who stare right through people,
hearing nothing from the musical
tones of cell phones,
programmed for the perceptive;
no, warnings are nothing
to city folk; they sit with cheerios
dripping from gums too tight
to chew, not understanding the air
they breathe, the noise they
hear, the rot-gutting
alcohol they slosh
down throats too eager
for pain.

Impeach Him

numbers trickle in.
the vote seems close,
but no matter,
the dark secrecy
of oil power
gurgles
in Texas.

lonesome doves perch
and flap,
skullduggery digs
deep, looking for
scandal.

they'll impeach if
he wins,
be sure.
they'll dig deeper
than Clinton,
lower than Lewinsky,
meaner than Cheney's
bitch-slapped dog.

the left will
hug trees to death;
the right will
actually go for
the jugular.

City Council

it's dark inside,
when you try to recoil
from words
shouted down the hall.
each shout rankles,
stirs up the primitive,
but being small
makes
a good target,
and being small carries
obligations like a cocked gun.
shooting off your own
mouth seems right,
but the flow
of history entices.
what's the use
of fighting
back when it takes
so little
to comply?

Oil

been to Texas,
studied film,
the Selznick years
at UT-Austin,
the beautiful capitol city,
so laid back,
like an ocean island cut out of
rock, the scary Dallas to the
north, and Vidor
with its KKK not far east.

but Austin has the Drag,
its parks,
the jogging trail
juiced up by Lady Bird's
flowers, the butterflies
swooping silently,
furtively,
protecting delicate
wings.

and for long moments,
the mean, short-haired bastards
retreat home,
waiting for the next
liberal-pinko-commie
rat to walk by.

then baseball bats, pinged

with power,
they'll swing and crush
skulls, no matter
how smart, how tender.
how hopeful the brain was
inside.

No Birth Control Today

the new evangelical pharmacist
has a wide smile, happy that he can stop us
from purchasing our birth control pills.
his sappy, god-loves-me face peers
through the glass window as we wait,
prescriptions in hand, scraping mud from our shoes
on white linoleum, inching our way
toward his assistants, who in their white
smocks resemble automatons, smiling
wide smiles, eyes blissed-out rapturously, awaiting
the split in the blue sky
that will yank them to heaven.
meanwhile, we stretch out our arms, giving up
the square prescriptions initialed by good doctors
celebrating birth control, allowing us
to love each other in our own bedrooms
with no consequences;
but the mad scientist rips the papers from our hands,
stamps them as received but refuses the pills,
saying his conscience prevents him from
such evil. and we slink away, back
to our pill dispensing doctors, who write
other prescriptions, other orders,
and we must wait for sex
until
some pharmacy, some K-Mart
hires a pharmacist without that
evil, religious smirk
of doom, judging us as sinners,

desiring each sperm and each egg
to mate and form unwanted
human life.

Presidential Pardon

only in some angel sky
lapped with gravy
can humans find
souls of feathered
creatures so deep
we can't speak their
language.

only their gobbling do we
recognize,
their other emotions
exasperate interpretation
except for those scientists
who probe
other clucks
and wheezes for deeper meaning.

yet each year one
is saved, by
presidential pardon,
one so plump,
so gobble-de-good
his plumpitude so
excruciatingly yummy
that our high-office
holder only burps
and lets the ungainly
drumsticks survive.

other turk-aliens are not
so lucky,
their limbs
loosed by humid heat,
till white meat and dark
lie carved in mounds
too delicious for burps,
too tender
for tomorrow.

Mart-Mart

quick sales and a western breeze
promise victory at the Mart-Mart,
the parking lot askew with training wheels
no one quite sure where to stop,
all yellow lines crooked
revealing a pattern to helicopters overhead
but granny drivers and grass-mowing junkies
seem confused,
the mulch pile
a dead-end, no hocus-pocus now,
just slim, stooping men
clad in jean jackets moving around inside,
suggesting leaf blowers
to hot-air aficionados,
their silver carts begging for utensils, pillow cases, junk
        food,
steering wheel gizmos that twirl,
red then purple, one non-stop checker
scanning coupons for last year's plastic swimming pools
rolled up in aisle five for young marrieds
carrying their kids in side cars attached
to tiny motorcycles all the fashion now,
riffing loud exhaust burps,
but tired grandpas sit in recliners
trying out adjustments to promised bliss,
each electric switch cascading pleasure
to extremities grown like pretzels
at the carnival.

Iraq Flashback

much concerned by midnight
bites
I toss out of bed,
slip on shoes,
explore my arms and legs.

Most surfaces seem pale,
but red blotches itch,
cream steroids smoothed
on.

Lights flicked
angrily bright,
sheets yanked to floor,
black spider emerges.

As big as my hand,
it struts,
jaws wide.

Stopped,
I grab long white
sword
and pierce the black inkiness
thrusting deeply.

Corpse with eight
legs wriggles
deadly,

venom dripping,
my agonizing scream
breaking the ozone.

Iraqi Kids

dusty dirt roads
huge army on the march
looking to kill.

up the hill
through the city,
mines line each bump,
each device ready.

driver steady,
his emotions cooled,
but crowds of kids
kick soccer balls in streets
just over hill's crest.

no time to stop, no rest
in war; the Humvee clatters,
trying to avoid
Iraqi kids, wearing only shorts
and smiles.

it'll take miles
of ocean cruises,
miles of Ozark trips before
the sergeant forgets.

bets are off in war,
the splintered, the bloodied,
the kids of war

splattered,
the Humvee's grill festooned
with guts.

and little, smiling kids squish,
their bodies once full of life,
their brains full of soccer scores,
crowding the dusty streets,
blocking in their innocence
a war they cannot avert.

Nuclear Clock

magazine's location
of the famous clock,
plots disasters,
mistakes and cleans dust
from every spot.
we behold our limits
and we invent
the ways.
do we long for last explosions,
the end of humans' race?

Thirsting for Oil

the foreign nation of the gas mobile,
its sides wrapped in steel,
its surface slick and slippery,
its innards thirsting, groaning,
the wheel turning , not resisting,
doomed prices rise
collectively,
each dappled sign
propelling costs obscenely
out of sight.
so when we learn
conservation,
we must accept
profoundly,
god-like reckoning
urging:
fuel is priceless,
walking, running, lost
arts,
and bicycles remain
with baskets
our only
frugal carts.

***

Oh, Holy Night

Jeffrey was running late again and I was getting pissed. His mother had

specially arranged everything with the Harrisons and Jeffrey was supposed to ride with them, but he messed up again. He never told us about his angel wings, so we had to drive across town, pick them up and then deliver them to the church right before midnight Mass, if we were lucky.

Angel wings for god's sake. Me and Beth didn't even know if the lady would

charge them for us. Shit. But the Harrisons were beeping their god damn horn, Jeffrey was in tears cuz I hollered at him, and Beth was ticked off at me for being so mean.

"See ya, Jeffy. Things will be all right," his mom was comforting him with

words. Meanwhile, Jeffrey looked in no shape to be in the procession, much less wear angel wings.

"Hurry up, Beth. We gotta go. Put him in the car. I'll start up the Nash. It's got

the reliable battery. Jen. Rose. Come with me. We gotta go get angel wings."

Well, Beth soon enough calmed down, I got the old black Nash started and we

were off on our journey across town to Front Street near downtown to see some lady about purchasing the wings. Jen and Rose were calmed down now, knowing I was in a bad mood. It was a real silent night as we drove down Bancroft to Cherry to the downtown Toledo, which was still all dressed up in Christmas splendor at 11 p.m. We had exactly one hour to make a deal, get back in the car and meet Jeffrey right before midnight Mass.

"Angel wings, for Chrissakes! Why didn't that damn teacher send a note
home? Then we coulda been prepared. She should know kindergarten kids forget things."

"Hush, Darrell. Just hush. Don't get the kids upset now. We'll get the wings
in no time. Don't worry."

Luckily, the streets were clear all the way to Cherry Street and I looked at my
watch. 11:10. Looked like we'd make it.

The address on Front was supposed to be 749 Front Street, but I couldn't see
the numbers and neither could Beth. Jen and Rose were still quiet. They could have helped but were afraid to try, I guess.

"Jen. Rose. You look too. I can't see the address so you guys look. 7.. 4... 9. Look for that address."

Soon we did make out a number in the pitch darkness but it was 311. We must
have gone right by the right address.

"God in heaven, help us find these damn angel wings," I bellowed. Shit, I was
using all this obscene language on Christmas Eve, in front of my two little daughters but I could damn care less. Shit. Angel wings for Chrissakes.

"There it is, Dad," said Jen.

"What? Where?"

"Right there, Dad. That grey house."

I stopped the Nash, got out and walked across the street. Yep. It was 749 Front all right but no one was home, there were no lights on, and they must be asleep.

I wasn't gonna stop now. I bolted up the stairs and commenced to ring the bell

while I was knocking the hell out of the door. "Hey, anyone home? We need angel wings. Hey. Answer your door."

I was upset until I saw a small light click on inside. A little Polish lady, I

swear, four feet tall, answered the door in some red felt nightie or something. She was still asleep, looking at me with dazed eyes. "Vat do you vant, son?" she asked me.

"Angel wings. For my son. For the procession. It's Christmas Eve and I need

to get some wings."

"Did you order any?" she asks.

"No, I don't know. My kid never told us about angel wings. We just need

some. Look I'll borrow some and return them tomorrow if you want."

"No, no, no. I no dose kids. Dey vill mess them up. You must pay $15.00

like everyone else."

"Fine. Fine. I'll pay on Friday when I get paid."

"No, sir. I'm very sorry. Cash only. I don't know you. You cannot have

credit."

"Listen, lady. I need those wings. What do you want? Should I give you one

of my daughters until Friday? Then I'll come get her and pay you? What do you want? I'm broke till Friday."

169

"Sir, you must wait. Wait till I talk vit my husband."

Well, she tottered away and I paced on the front porch, looking over at Beth in

the car, shaking my head back and forth. My watch now said 11:30. If we get the wings right now we might make it on time.

The little lady returned with two golden wings made out of something like tree

decorations, icicles, whatever you call them. She showed me just the tip of one wing, but I got the idea.

"Yeah. Yeah. So are you gonna give em to me? I got to go now. Mass starts in

twenty-five minutes. Please."

She was mumbling something about how to put them on and how to store them

and how to hold them above the ground so they don't get dirty. And I was saying, "Thank you, thank you, yes, yes, thank you, I'll see you on Friday and Merry Christmas to you and your husband. Merry Christmas."

Back in the car I threw the wings in the back seat, right on top of Rose, started

the Nash and we rambled off into the night.

It was 11:40.

I gave it the gas and laid a pile of rubber stinking up Front Street all the way to

Cherry. Then down Bancroft to Parkside Blvd. and all the lights were on in the church and the whole congregation was parking their cars on every side street in every sort of parking disorder.

Instead of parking in front, I swung around next to the cemetery fence and

raced to the back of the church where I knew all the

kids would be lining up to go inside. Beth is screaming at me to slow down and Jen and Rose are now crying, and Rose is screaming something about the wings getting crushed.

I parked right near the rectory, tell Beth to meet me just outside the church

entrance. Then I grabbed those god-damn angel wings and run like a bat or angel out of heaven all the way to the end of the procession where Jeffrey is sitting down. He's not allowed in the procession without angel wings, one of the nuns tells me.

I said, "Well, here. Help me put em on Jeffrey, Sister." So she slides or glides

over toward me, looks at the wings and says, "These are not angel wings for the boys. This is a set of girls' angel wings."

Well, I lost it right there and said, "Sister, if God and Baby Jesus and all the

Wise Men and St. Joseph object, then I don't know what. Get these wings on Jeffrey. I'm not gonna argue the finer points."

Well, dear Sister Elizabeth or Isabel, one of the two, kind of gives me a very,

very wicked look, but she does put the wings over Jeffrey's shoulders and slides the tape together properly and no one's gonna care.

So Jeffrey is fairly happy, but I hear him say, "I'm not a girl."

So I just tell him to be a good Christian and sing loud.

Now I notice I'm out of breath, but Beth is waving to me, so I rush over to the entrance. Beth fixes my tie properly and dusts my jacket and we enter the church.

But there are no seats. Only in the balcony. We're so late we climb the stairs to

the balcony and have to sit in the middle of the back row, behind the choir. We cannot see the altar. We cannot see the procession.

But those children's voices. Those little kindergarten voices are so sweet the

tears come to my eyes and I thank the Blessed Savior for making me a god-fearin' Catholic.

***

Part 4 Sports Page

*My first tennis practices were against
the wall on the east side of the Ottawa
Tavern building. This brick wall was not
forgiving, and my serve and forehand
were grooved hitting each evening.
At the time I didn't know that Mrs. Jean Hoxie.
up in Hamtramck, Michigan, had a tennis
school which made walls like these the
major component of her teaching. Many
great tennis players were turned out up
there in Detroit. My skills were honed
enough against my red brick wall, so that
I could play tennis on St. Francis' first
tennis team. Later, I went to Toledo University
and played varsity three years.*

***

Darts at Ottawa Park

let's just say
in the middle of this timely letter
say one thing
about friends and
why you left
that sunny day
park swing still
moving the pond
glittering the bright
sun mostly tightly yellow
with mustard flowers blooming so
what if no one
but me
noticed
you were still
way gone
back marching
through parking lots
pick-up trucks scooting nearby
looking for empty spots
before my eyes
you loved
me so you said
and then
and then
bitter dandelion taste
tongues burning
with hate
cactus plants flinging
darts.

Visit

shutting our eyes we see the moment,
the door opening, the car shut down.
he emerges fresh, though the drive
over mountains fatigued softly,
like a morning mist settling
on copper before turning green.
any dust he flicks off his shoulders
encased in polyester sweats,
a style suited for long trips,
autumn's chill, winter's
cringing cold.
he grips our hands, claps backs,
a football coach greeting lost teammates
after twenty years of mold.
into the house we go,
he pausing by the porch swing,
one swift memory of summer song,
of girls held tight
at midnight's hour.
inside we grab hotdogs and beer,
the laughter muted by years
we never shared.

We Meet Sports Guy

We had one kid in the neighborhood
who was always a more dedicated
golfer than other neighbor kids.
We'd practice putting near the S. P.
Jermain statue in the middle
of the putting green at Parkside and Bancroft,
and then tee off at Ottawa Park, hitting
the ball across the park road directly
at the bottom of the first tee. A good drive
avoided Ten-Mile Creek, but a slice
would lose you a ball. The future pro always
hit practice balls, dead serious about
his game. I think he was the only one
of us that would go to the park with a
bag of balls just to practice. The rest of us
only liked to play. At that time it was twenty-five
cents for eighteen holes during the week.
One time an older guy played in our foursome.
We all knew who he was from television
sports news, but he introduced himself
anyway. He said, "Hello. I'm Frank Venner."

Eight Ball

orange and fair our skin,
next to keeping house,
our dreams vibrate,
our nocturnal pleasures
eerily oblique, those motions
toward the sun reciprocated
by furry animals looking for love,
looking for universal truths,
while all we do
is push vacuum sweepers noisily
up the stairs,
plodding
toward bathrooms,
much too dirty for guests,
our holiday friends waiting
in basements, having
only the eight ball
to knock around on pool tables,
cue sticks chalked
too harshly,
chalk dust covering carpets,
while we scramble
to dust the bookshelves,
hiding our copies
of John O'Hara lest
some guest notice
our thoughts.

Homeruns at The Dump

Behind our duplex at 1924 Freeman were
two former city dumps. One was between
Freeman and Macomber. The other was
between Macomber and Milburn. We called
these dumps the "first dump" and the "second dump."
The first dump was right across the alley
from our back yard. It was all filled in, but had
small hills of trash covered over by high grass.
City mowers would cut this grass in the dump
maybe two times a year. When they did, we
played softball in the first dump, using the
fences behind our homes as homerun fences.
Funny to think of this now, but one neighbor
had a wonderful garden and
he patrolled it when he was home. Then it
was dangerous to hit a long ball. Our biggest hitter
simply killed the ball and many
times we tried to get his homeruns back.
After a homerun, we would have to sneak
into the garden. However, when the gardener
was there, he would confiscate our softballs
and never give them back. When he died
many years later, I visited my old home
and went to his Estate Sale. There in his
garage were all of our old, moldy softballs,
about ten, that he had confiscated. It was
like a scene out of the movie "Birdy,"
when one of the characters played by

*Matt Modine is tempted out of his mental
illness by the delivery of old softballs
kept by his mother.*

Fort Meigs Sport

old Indian trails traced
fields. the nearby ruts of wagons
pushed west
toward the distant mountains, the plains folk
wrapped in blankets watching
desperate pilgrims escape
cities, trading comfort
for pain.

this evening history seems near,
our own straw-covered floor pitching
as rubber wheels roll over earth's clefts,
our search for orange gourds bringing
laughter to the younger ones
sitting at the edge,
dangling feet toward moving history.

beneath the dry grass
lurk arrowheads and fangs,
mixed together in tumult,
a frenzy of frozen rage,
the pumpkins spurting out
like ruptures
from battle sores
in fields,
the gasps recognized
only for their intensity,
forgotten warriors struggling
with blood in their throats,
ghosts chilling the air.

Mud Hen Baseball

kiss your lips with
my popcorn cheese mouth,
each taste a liquid of desire
on two levels,
each kernel like first base,
each cheesy lump
a surrogate for second,
and third is as easy
as a slide trombone
in coca-cola,
sweet, bubbly
with sounds of escape,
my home run
coming later,
like a forgotten
puffed crunch,
surprising yet
filling you up.

Morning Jog at Wildwood

our jogging path is morbid,
yet quiet in the morning fog.

each tombstone thrusts
its lost hours
into dreamy mist.

our footfalls echo against death,
our quiet talk about life
ends, our breath visible
in floating smoke.

we pass the famous
dead, their plots large
and kept with yellow mums.

someone placed fresh flowers
for these lonesome friends,
but mums turn brown
and bend to ground.

we turn toward exits now,
leaving ghosts behind,
the murmurs not our own,
those chronic coughs
barking at us
like sad dogs
chained to concrete posts.

Ottawa Hills Tennis

One memorable tennis match occurred when
I was a freshman at Central High School,
the year before I transferred to St. Francis
to become a member of the first graduating
class of 1958. There was a tournament at
Jermain Park, and I drew the first man from
Ottawa Hills H. S. in the first round. Within
a half hour, I had lost, 6—0, 6—0. During
breaks, the guy would juggle tennis balls
for his own amusement to my chagrin.
It was the only time I played him.
Later at St. Francis when we played Ottawa
Hills, our coach switched our line-up, playing
me at number three singles and another
weaker player was sacrificed.
I won my match, but we still lost to
Ottawa Hills, 3—2. Not playing the number
one player embarrassed me. It's not considered
sporting to adjust a tennis team line-up that way.

Aurora at Fremont Speedway

twisted
minds foggy with cold,
wind currents approach
Nascar speeds and dizziness
commences outside tents
flopped by temperatures
knifing exposed skin;
each miniature tent-thread
torn asunder
spelling doom;
outside
ice crystals form on eyelids,
exposure just split-seconds
away from comprehension;
the beauty of reds, greens,
sky-pinks glow and glint,
electrical energy
speeding through
the universe,
but latching onto
cold mountains
to terrify explorers
bent-nasty
in their bedrolls,
keeping warm.

Battle at the Paintball Coliseum

he went alone
that night
quite solemn but full
of his ego
caressing that voice
that complained
for the voice knew danger
knew exactly what the night
could bring
its cautious warning
louder each step
he took.

Fast-Pitch Softball

My father, Palmer Sheldon Rochelle, was a very
good athlete. He pitched for the Plaskon fast-pitch
softball team, throwing sinkers, curves, innies and
outies, and not using a mitt to field the balls coming
back at him. He also played a nifty game of golf,
batting cross-handed. His softball games often were
played at the CYO field across from the golf course.
I watched him many times and got to know
some of the players. The team was very good,
and played at least once against
Eddie Feigner's four man team.

CYO Football

kitchen supplies and flour,
a dusting, no more
no less an ocean of aroma,
and into this tumult
came a boy,
his hands grimy
from football, his wishes
on instant response;
to get back
to his friends
a force, but other
primitive juices
called: apples, pears,
fresh-baked dough.

The Cave on North Cove

kids and mud
resistible to adults
but their old digging fingers
have typed or doodled
too long for the fun
of deep adventure.

assaying the ground,
and imaging results,
the kids strike out,
implements held tight
and engineering skills
creating dreams.

a farm, a cave
worthy of Huck Finn,
just enough height
for entrance
letting three inside,
while one imp watches
for anxious moms who
hope for ceilings
strong for creatures
who still yearn
for comfort
from warm cocoa
and graham crackers.

Old-Timer at Jermain

While spending most of my afternoons and
evenings at Jermain Park, I came to respect
the good tennis players there. An older player
also haunted those courts. He would always
be looking for a game of singles after he
got off work, and if I could finish my paper
route quickly, I could just get down there in time
to play him. He still wore those long, white or
tan pants from the 1930s tennis era with a
regular short-sleeved white shirt. His style
very smooth, his backhand still the best on
those courts even if he was losing some steam.
Some of the younger players teased him,
especially after they learned to beat him.
He had an utterly fascinating way of looking
at you when you hit a winner, and then
he'd say, "I don't believe it."

Nocturnal Sport

doubling back under trees dripping
rain, the beast hid waiting.
night walkers passed, their scuffling
Nikes picking up mud, debris.
listening, the beast skirted the fir tree
and hunched its shoulders,
letting fear palpitate,
and scatter.
one motion and it could
kill, slashing out
with claws ripping flesh.
but it waited, hidden
in the suburban night,
while a CD played its rap.

Ace, The Friendly Dog

All of us loved animals
and we adopted a neighbor dog named "Ace."
He was a traveler and would follow us
everywhere, even on the golf course as we
played. We finally gave this dog a longer
name, "Ace, the Friendly Dog," because
wherever he went, he made friends. There
was no leash law back then. Another dog
named "Ace" belonged to our neighbors
and was kept in a pen. It was a hunting dog
and used to chasing and pointing. However,
one day it escaped the pen and took off
after us, growling. We all ran away, and
only I was left to outrace this dog. I made
it behind our garage to the tree with a low
limb, but as I climbed up, the hunting dog
Ace bit my butt.

Yearbook Mob

I placed the high school keepsake carefully
on the dining room table, letting all
the leaves release so we could sit
close and share.
the football photo we wanted was as ever,
the squat face, the small eyes,
the look of evil humor, wicked
in senior class, evil when flashed
after that night he stole the car.
then today's newspaper crackled to page two,
metro news, another photo:
a moustache now, wrinkles
on his forehead, long hair at the side
with bare skin on top.
but the eyes were the same, cold,
distant, no mirth now,
just the evil of crime, of escape,
of the need to resist.

Hunter's Perch

violent images and a long sigh,
those watching seemed bitten off by flight,
each feather plucked and floating,
vile actions misinterpreted, giving instant release.

when feathers flew, marksmen tottered eerily,
motion suspended, blast in ears
absolute, and a fear rising.

if faces seemed dull, seemed still,
wasn't it a tightness, a belly-cramp, a serious
regret, with the blue tufts of reality
lilting, slipping into silence?

Ottawa Park Sledding

side by side
contestants jockey
looking into the white
flakes of speed.

each resting vertically
feet encased in boots
fingers gripping
wood ready for release.

paths of ice glitter
while most tots
clear out
the demons possess
these speedsters.

on signal mates
pump up their courage
and shove off
danger flying past
as dark tree trunks
menace and fresh
flakes fall.

Jermain Park Industrial League

*My dad's tennis game was a thing of exotic
beauty. A chunky 5' 8", dad was very muscular,
but had a finesse game. He undercut the
ball on most of his strokes, giving the ball
tremendous torque. He could spin it to
either side. His regular serve was adequate,
but his underhand serve was sheer terror.
Most tennis players avoid the underhand
serve (thinking it's underhanded?), but dad
perfected it, moving the ball to left or right
or to an almost dead stop. A very effective
serve in doubles, and he was the Industrial
League champ. We played at Jermain.
Dad was also excellent at horseshoes, and
Jermain had the soft, wet clay necessary
for good play. The clay was tended carefully,
and dad pitched ringers and taught
us the game. It's hard to find good
clay horseshoe courts like that today.*

***

Getting to Westminster

It was already ten-thirty and the car wouldn't start. I had been through this a
million times, but I kept waiting for the one time that the engine would crank over.

"Jon, get out here and help push the beast again, will ya? Just today. I'm late
for the game and the team will be there and I won't."

"Jessuz. Will you just buy another car? No one drives a '39 Willys
anymore. The War's over. Get yourself a good car."

"Sure, sure, with what money? Now, come on. Get up. I gotta go."

Jon rolled over one more time and prepared his head for sleep under the
covers, but I took that beat up old broom of mine and gave his rear a whack that could be heard all the way to Ottawa Park. "Get up. I don't ask for much but you could at least get out of bed before noon."

Jon was staying in our front spare bedroom. Actually the room was technically
a sunroom in the sense that it had windows all around, it let in the sun and it was extremely hot in the summer and in the winter snow could blow in from the cracks in the walls. Of course, Jon didn't have to pay us nothin', but me and Sherry didn't mind too much, as long as he got up once in a while and gave me a push.

Now I had Jon's attention, but he turned sullen on me. He was sullen when he put on his socks, sullen when he put on his pants, sullen when he put on his shoes.

Jon had attitude before attitude became popular.

"Listen, you son of a bitch. You hit me with that broom again and I'll kill your
ass."

Yup, Jon was perturbed all right, but he had his car keys and he was heading
out the front door. I followed a few steps back, still belligerent myself but unwilling to trade blows with Jon just yet. Maybe after my car started.

The Willys sat in the driveway, facing the wrong way, so me and Jon starting
pushing it down the slight incline down to the street, and I deftly hopped in the driver's side once it got movin' good. I swung out backwards into the street and stopped, so the car could go forward with the natural flow of the street.

Jon revved up the engine on his '47 Chevy, put it in gear and crept close to the
back bumper of the Willys, ready to push me. We had a short block to get the car goin' about twenty mph, and then maybe it'd kick in when I let out the clutch. I never knew for sure if the first push would do it, but I was hoping.

The bumpers connected just about perfectly so Jon started out slow to make
sure of a constant shove effect. Neither of us wanted to bounce against the other, although a good bounce wouldn't really hurt the Willys. Jon was just afraid of damaging his front grill.

Soon, we were at twenty mph, I kicked in the clutch; the cold engine fought back, slowed us down, but then came to life. It didn't roar to life, it sort of sputtered and coughed and wheezed to life.

I gave Jon the thumbs up sign and whirled right through the stop sign, not willing to risk stopping until the old car modulated its engine. I could see Jon pull into the Robinson's driveway and turn around to go back. Meanwhile, I buzzed up to Bancroft, looked both ways, and cut out east into the road, heading for the downtown Westminster gym. If I drove hard and made the lights, I'd get there in time to give some instructions to my Gesu team.

I chugged along Monroe Street, the wind whistling through the plastic I had put over the door window. I had trouble with rolling the windows up in the car, and in the night the clothes pin I used as a wedge between the window and the car door had come loose, causing the glass to drop to the bottom. It always happened that way. The other window on the passenger side stayed up probably because I used three clothes pins for wedges.

There was a mess of cars parked on the street outside the gym, and I had to park on an incline, just to make sure I could get the car started after the game. I'd had the players push me one other time, and the eight of them got me up to ten mph on a hill, which was just enough for me to pop the clutch and get it started. So, I parked on 18th Street facing west, so I'd have about two blocks of space to get it started later.

Inside, the gym noise echoed in the big hall. Formerly a church, Westminster gym had only a short three-tiered grandstand on one side, with folding chairs for the players at either end. Toward the middle of the opposite side were the tables for the official scorers and the timer.

I looked up at the clock and noticed that the game before ours was runnin' late. Must be in overtime or somethin'. The clock read, 0u.48. Some of the lights were out so I guessed that the "u" was actually a zero, so the game had just 48 seconds to go. The score was St. Thomas 40 and St. Ann's 35. Pretty high scoring game for a bunch of eighth grade kids.

I heard some incessant bouncing of a basketball and thought only one person,

our nervous team captain, Bobbie Funk, and sure enough it was Bobby bouncing that named ball against a wall on the other end. He was being obnoxious as usual and the two refs seemed annoyed with him.

"Hey, Kid. Stop that bouncing. Put the ball down," they yelled.

Bobby looked up from his nervous tension focus, and said, "Who me?" But at

least he stopped that racket.

I jogged over to him and the rest of my team, all except Bobby sitting on the

floor in the end zone area, rooting for St. Ann's to win. They were the easier team, so we'd play them next and kill them. But the score indicated that they would lose. And they did.

I hung my jacket on a spike on the wall, gathered the team around me and

handed out the game shirts. We had six shirts, but eight players, so two players would have to trade shirts to get in the game. Just last week I had Ace Gooden go in the game late in the fourth quarter, but he put his head in the arm hole and had to play about two minutes incapacitated, cause both his head and his right arm were in the same hole. He looked real funny, and only after a time out could we get him unhooked. Good thing we had a fifteen point lead.

I called out the starters' names, "Bobby, Arrow, Dick, Olson, and Doug,"

then we gathered in our tight little circle, said our Hail Mary, yelled a loud, "Beat, 'em, Beat 'em" and took the floor to face the enemy, Nativity from the tough section of town. All Polacks, Nativity was known for dirty street type ball, strong profanity, and tough rebounding. Our team was all finesse and passing, lay-ups and ball stealing. Nativity hated us because we were mostly Irish and rich.

For the next hour or so, both teams pounded the loose wooden boards, traded

baskets, and caused a lot of turnovers. Bobby was hot from the outside, his set-shot was a high arcing beauty, and we pulled off a win by three points. Ace was not happy with me. "Coach, why didn't you put me in? We had a lead. We had a lead and you wouldn't put me in."

All I said was "maybe next time" and I could not tell Ace that we needed at

least a fifteen point lead before I could put him in. He was just too risky. And the other kids would hate me if I put him in and we lost. So, Ace usually sat on the bench.

And, of course, Ace had no one to drive him home so I volunteered. All the other dads and moms took their kids home, but I was stuck with Ace. Not that I minded that much. He was a good kid, just uncoordinated.

Back at the Willys, both Ace and I pushed it down the incline and jumped

inside as it picked up steam. I let the clutch out and it chugged once, twice, and then started. Both of us whooped it up, "Yeah, all right, way to go."

Back home, I asked Ace if he was hungry. I had a special treat for him. I

walked over to the trunk of Jon's car, hit the key area and popped the trunk lid. Inside, Jon had a bunch of old candy boxes which he couldn't sell, and most of the chocolates had turned white, but they were still edible I guess. I shoved a box of coconut bon-bons at Ace and he opened them up and just smiled that divine smile of his. "God, Frankie, look at all the candy."

He was pleased. I said that he deserved a treat for sitting on the bench all the

time and practicing hard.

He looked up and seemed to understand. He walked away to his home across

the large vacant lot and hollered back at me, "Thanks, Coach. See ya on Tuesday for practice."

I went inside our apartment and noticed Jon was back in bed. God, I wished my

wife would get home from her sister's.

***

Larry Rochelle is a Toledo native and a tennis bum. He also was a newsboy for The Toledo Blade. Presently, he teaches English Composition and Cinema at Johnson County Community College in Kansas.

Other books by Larry Rochelle available at http://Booksurge.com

POETRY:

"Dust Devils" *Kansas Nelson Poetry Book of the Year 2004*

"Siren Sorcery" *Eppie Finalist 2005*

"Pistol Whipped"

THE PALMER MOREL MYSTERY SERIES

"Dance with the Pony" *Cincinnati "City Beat's" Book of the Year 2003*

"The Mephisto Diary"

"Cracked Crystals" *Eppie Finalist 2005*

"TraceTracks"

"Bourbon and Bliss"

"Death and Devotion"

EDUCATION

"Prof Rap"

Made in the USA